D0567379

Pet Owner's Guide to
THE
GERMAN SHEPHERD
DOG
Dr. Malcolm B. Willis

RINGPRESS

RINGPRESS

Published by Ringpress Books Limited,
PO Box 8, Lydney, Gloucestershire
GL15 6YD, United Kingdom.

First Published 1993
Reprint 1996
© 1993 Ringpress Books Limited.
All rights reserved

ISBN 0 948955 33 3

Printed and bound in Hong Kong

Contents

About the author

Dr Malcolm B. Willis is Senior Lecturer in Animal Breeding and Genetics in the Faculty of Agriculture at the University of Newcastle upon Tyne.

Dr Willis bought his first German Shepherd in 1953 and has owned them ever since. He first judged in 1959, gave Challenge Certificates in 1978, and has judged in nine countries around the world. For some thirteen years he was on the Council of the GSD League, and he has been Chairman of the GSD Breed Council in Britain since it was formed in the mid 1980s. He is one of the ten breed surveyors for the Breed Council, and runs the genetic

side of the hip dysplasia scoring scheme for all breeds. In 1988 he was awarded a gold medal from the GSD Council of Australia for services to the breed, and that same year judged the 'GSD National' in Britain, the only Briton yet to do so. A prolific writer for numerous canine/breed publications, Dr Willis is author of two classic books on the breed, two books on canine genetics, and three on beef cattle and animal breeding. His book *The German Shepherd Dog: A Genetic History* won first prize in its class at the 1992 Dog Writers Association Of America awards. Dr Willis has lectured to canine groups, veterinarians and breed clubs throughout the world. He lives in Northumberland with his wife, Helen, who breeds Bernese Mountain Dogs, a breed in which both give CCs. They have nine dogs (2 GSD, and 7 BMD) and three British short-haired cats.
Author's note: Throughout the text, the abbreviation GSD has been used liberally to denote the German Shepherd Dog.

Acknowledgements

This book has been read and checked by my wife, Helen, whose suggestions have improved the text; any defects which remain must be laid at my door.
Thanks to those who have co-operated in taking photographs for this book, in particular: The Guide Dogs for the Blind Association, the Metropolitan Police, the New York Police Dept., members of the Welwyn/Hatfield branch of the British Association for GSDs, Daphne Rowe, Margaret Jones (Lodge, Kennels, Baldock, Herts), David and Rhoda Payne (Videx GSDs), Wendy and Graham Stephens (Ardenburg GSDs), and Roy and Clarissa Allan (Shootersway GSDs).
Cover photograph: Lufdarl Jarros (pet name Jaxon). Owned by Mrs Jennifer Griffin, bred by Mrs Daphne Rowe. Note that Jaxon has a tattoo in his ear. This is listed on a national register, so that if the dog ever went missing he could be identified and re-united with his owner.

The German Shepherd is used worldwide as a police dog.

Chapter One

SIMPLY THE BEST!

ORIGINS OF THE GERMAN SHEPHERD DOG

Most dog breeders like to imagine that their breed goes back into antiquity. In fact, as dog breeds go, the German Shepherd is relatively modern. Its origins go back to Germany and the last two decades of the 19th century. At that time there existed in Germany a number of German sheepdogs which were of very mixed appearance. There was a variety of colours ranging from wolf-grey through to white and even piebald. There were short, long and wire coats, and ears that were erect or dropped, as well as numerous other variations. In fact, these dogs were a mixture of types and a mixture of ancestry.

An unsuccessful attempt to set up a breed club was made in the late 1880s, but shortly afterwards a German cavalry officer called Max von Stephanitz established a society to seek to develop the mixed bag of German herding types into what, in German, was called the Deutsche Schaferhunde. Von Stephanitz was a rather opinionated individual, but he was undoubtedly a leader. It was he who was the driving force behind the club (the Verein fur Deutsche Schaferhunde or SV); he was behind the first Breed Standard, and he was the club's president from its start in 1899 until his death in 1936.

From the mixed types available, it was decided to select a dog that had a short coat (rather than long or wire), that had erect ears, and was of a dark colour. Most early dogs were wolf-grey, but black-and-tan, and black were also acceptable. White dogs were not accepted. Initially, size was variable, and males ranged from under 60 to 67cm (24-27in), while weight was light at around 28-36kg (62-79lb). The dog used as a prototype was Horand v Grafrath, who was owned by von Stephanitz, and Horand was registered as SZ 1. The letters SZ precede the number of any dog in the SV registration book or *Zuchtbuch*.

The SV made rapid strides, holding its first Sieger (Championship) show in 1899, and increasing membership at a rapid rate as the popularity of the new breed grew. The breed was, of course, a herding breed, but it demonstrated a considerable intelligence, and at the outbreak of World War One, the German Shepherd Dog or GSD, as it became abbreviated, was the 'war' dog of choice for the Kaiser's army. At that time the army dog used by the British was the Airedale Terrier, but with due respect to that breed, it did not have the qualities that made the GSD the ideal war dog. Prior to the 1914-18 war, the GSD had not extended very far outside Germany, although examples had reached the USA and Britain, as well as other European countries. After the war, many army officers returned home with examples of the breed, and thereafter its expansion was both dynamic and assured.

PUBLIC REACTION TO THE GSD

There are probably more German Shepherd Dogs in the world than any other pedigree breed of dog. In Germany, the GSD was – and still is – among the most popular breeds in numerical terms, and the SV is the world's largest breed club of any species. In Britain, the rise of the GSD after 1918 was meteoric. By 1926 GSD registrations with the KC were the most of any breed. There was some decline during the 1930s, but after 1946 the breed was again in top spot in numerical terms, and has been in the first three ever since. At present, some 16,000 GSDs are registered annually in Britain.

There was a similar pattern in USA, where the breed has generally been in the top ten, and where registrations per year now exceed 50,000. In most countries, it would be true to say that the GSD is among the most popular breeds where pedigree dogs are bred and exhibited. It is undoubtedly the most recognised breed of all, and though it has been extremely popular throughout its history, it has also been much maligned.

When the breed first came to Britain after the 1914-'18 war, it was much criticised as being a 'wolf dog'. In fact, the wolf is 'in' every dog since all derived from a type of wolf. In Australia the breed was so severely criticised that from the late 1920s through to the early 1970s the importation of GSDs was forbidden, and in most States punitive taxes had to be paid, while breeding was often banned. The ban was imposed in the belief that the GSD would mate with the Dingo and produce a formidable race of sheep killers.

Dogs do mate with Dingos, but there was no evidence that the GSD did so any more frequently than other dogs, and in any event, much of the criticism of Dingos is inaccurate. Despite this level of prejudice against the GSD, within a short time of the ban being lifted, the GSD was quickly the most popular breed in the country. The standard of quality of the breed in Australia is now among the best in the world, and has been achieved inside twenty years.

VERSATILITY OF THE BREED

The Shepherd is probably the most versatile of breeds. It may not be as good a tracker as the Bloodhound and, contrary to popular belief, it is not a particularly aggressive dog. It can, however, become very attached to, and protective of, its master and its master's property – as, indeed, the Breed Standard requires. Nevertheless, in all-round merit the GSD has no equal.

It is the best police dog, as can be seen by the fact that throughout the world it is the breed most often used by police, the armed services or para-military groups. It has been one of the most commonly used guide dogs for the blind, and if it is now giving way on this count to Labradors and Golden Retrievers, this is partly because of the greater stature of GSD, and also because GSD require more skilful and sensitive handling.

The original role of the GSD was to work sheep, and in Germany and elsewhere it is still to be found doing that job. It does not work like a Border Collie or a Kelpie, but that was not its role, and though its herding role has declined there are still bloodlines which can herd to perfection. As a guard dog, the very reputation serves it well and few dogs are as alert and watchful as a GSD. Some owners have used the GSD to work to the gun with considerable success, although its ear carriage is not suited to such work.

ABOVE:The breed's loyalty, intelligence, and protective instincts makes it ideal for police work.

LEFT: The GSD has an excellent nose, and so it can be employed for tracking and rescue work.

Guide Dogs for the Blind must have a calm, steady temperament, and GSDs were the first breed used for this work.

As an all-round dog, the GSD is probably the best there is, and most of us who have been bitten by the GSD bug would argue that there is no breed that is as beautiful to behold at an extended trot, or that is as versatile. The breed is such that once you have owned a GSD, then, for most people, there will be no other breed that will replace it in your affections. I have owned GSDs for forty years, and though I have owned and lived with a Newfoundland and with Bernese Mountain Dogs and derived great pleasure from them, the GSD is the finest breed I have known.

THE GSD COMMUNITY

In most countries where dogs are exhibited, the GSD community is very different from the rest of the dog show world. In the main, GSD enthusiasts want their breed judged by those judges who are 'in the breed' and are specialists, not judges associated with a multiplicity of other breeds. Most GSD owners want to watch their breed being judged, and when that is done they have little interest in cross-breed competition.

Those who work GSDs in other disciplines, such as Obedience, Working Trials, Schutzhund or in Agility are usually interested in that activity with GSD, and their loyalty will not change to some other breed, even if, as with Obedience, the system of judging favours other breeds. A Shepherd man is a Shepherd man, and that desire to stay with the breed is, in part, instigated by the breed's own virtues.

Though there are exceptions to any rule, the breeders of GSDs tend to be, as a group, more knowledgeable than most, and they are much more prepared than most to discuss the failings and defects which affect the breed. As a group, it was GSD breeders who pioneered hip dysplasia research and other features, just as they have pioneered Breed Surveys. If you join the GSD fraternity, you will be expected to go along with this type of policy.

Chapter Two

YOUR NEW PUPPY

The majority of breeders let their puppies go from seven to eight weeks of age, and in most cases the puppy will be collected by the new owners. The exception would be when the pup has to undergo a long journey – in countries such as the USA and Australia, where distances are far greater – and the puppy may have to be shipped by air.

PREPARATIONS
A few days before you are due to collect your puppy, check with the breeder to find out exactly what diet is being fed, and make sure that you purchase the same type of food in advance. Remember that the puppy has to face the trauma of leaving the only home he has known, being separated from his siblings and his mother, plus making a journey either alone by air, or in a car. This is enough to upset any puppy, and the last thing he wants on top of this is a change of diet.

THE JOURNEY
If your puppy is being shipped by air, check that you have the right airport, the flight number, and the time of arrival. Make sure you are there on time, with a travelling cage, so you can take your puppy home by car, completing the long journey with the least possible delay.

If you are going by car to collect your puppy, it is better to take someone with you to either hold the pup, or, better still, take a travelling cage. The puppy can then be put in the cage and placed on the back seat alongside your friend or yourself, depending on who is driving. If you cannot recruit a friend and you are collecting the puppy on your own, the travelling cage is almost essential. I have known puppies travel on their first journey next to the driver, but it is potentially dangerous, especially if the puppy is lively.

If the journey is relatively short, an hour or so, then the puppy can probably make the journey without a stop. If the journey is lengthy, then a stop to give the puppy water may be necessary. The pup may want to relieve himself, but do not let him out of the car as he is not fully vaccinated. Let him relieve himself in the travelling crate, which you should have lined with old newspapers. You can clean up on arrival at home. If you must stop en route, pull into a service station rather than stopping on the roadside. Accidents can happen and agile puppies escape very easily – so do not be near a road.

You should travel equipped with a bowl, and a plastic bottle or thermos-flask full of fresh water. Your puppy can thus have a drink, which he may well need to avoid some element of dehydration, depending upon the weather. Be gentle all the time: when you pick the puppy up, lifting him out of the box, and in the car. Do not let the puppy jump. Unless the journey is really lengthy, do not feed him as the pup could well be sick if he is unused to car travel. If the car makes him sick then ensure that he does drink.

ARRIVING HOME
When you get your puppy home you can offer some food, though he may be disinterested. Although he is now home and safe on your premises, do not start getting him involved in lots of play. The puppy will be tired and stressed, even if he is of excellent character, so let him rest or, if he chooses, trot around after you as you do your household chores. Do not overtire your puppy. Show him his bed, and make sure he can lie down when he wants to. If you are using a crate, introduce the pup to the crate, and when you think he needs a rest, crate him. Give the puppy a toy to play with, or offer a large marrow bone to keep him occupied.

THE FIRST NIGHT
The first night may be a noisy one. The puppy may well cry, and you will be tempted to go down and see to him. Resist the temptation, unless you think the pup has got into some problem. The type of noise should tell you whether anything is actually wrong. If you suspect a problem, observe the puppy from a distance, preferably unobserved. If all is well, leave the puppy alone. If the pup is crated, he has less chance of getting into trouble than if he is just in a dog bed. If there is no problem and you go to your puppy he will be quiet – but he will start up again as soon as you leave him. Your first night, even the first few nights, may be disturbed by a crying puppy but leave him alone or you will set a precedent that will be even harder to correct. Let your puppy out to relieve himself last thing at night and first thing in the morning, and go with him. Make a fuss of your puppy each morning, and when he relieves himself outside.

FEEDING
Feed your puppy as instructed by the breeder, and *do not change the diet* because the pup does not seem to like it. This is the food the puppy has been eating previously, and he will again. However, not all breeders feed ideal diets. If you have reason to suppose that the diet is not ideal and you wish to change it, do this gradually, over a period of a few days. The best way of doing this is to use a mixture of the old diet and the new diet, and then gradually reduce the original feed, and increase the new diet.

HEALTH CHECK
Many breeders in the UK insure their puppies for six weeks or even longer, although this is not common practice in the USA. If you are a one-dog owner it is probably wise to renew that insurance before it expires, but if you have many dogs it may not be economical to insure. However, within forty-eight hours of purchase make sure that you take your puppy to your veterinarian to have him checked over. If the puppy is ill or has any serious defect, you should consider returning him... take your vet's advice.
  The breeder should have supplied you with details of worming programmes, and

whether the vaccination programme has been started. Your vet will tell you what vaccinations are necessary, and when to return for them. While you are at the vet's surgery do not put your puppy down, keep him on your lap and do not go near other dogs.

THE NEXT FEW WEEKS

I am assuming that, having bought a puppy, at least one member of your household is at home during the day. If not, then your puppy will have a fairly traumatic experience and do not be surprised if, during your absences, he proves to be destructive unless crated. If you are not at home then buying a puppy is questionable, but having done so, at least ensure that he is given lots of attention when you are at home – but do not over-fuss him. You have bought a GSD, not a toy, so do not constantly fuss and cuddle him.

Let your puppy follow you and be around you, and tickle his ears or his belly, but try to stop him jumping up, and do not let him sit on the furniture. Play with your puppy by all

A puppy has lots of experiences to get used to in its new home.

means, going down on the floor with him and trying retrieving and other active games, but do not tire him out. A puppy will still play long after he has really had enough. Use your judgement on this count. Above all, get your puppy used to his name and to coming to you when called – but like all training, do not do things to excess.

In the next few weeks your puppy will be teething and the mouth will be sore. Do not constantly maul your puppy's mouth to check on his teeth. Remember, too, that during teething, ear carriage is often erratic. Groom regularly using a soft brush, and on a weekly basis check on ears, but do not pour things into ears as you can do more harm by messing about with ears than by leaving them alone. The erect ear carriage of the GSD tends to bring fewer problems than soft ears, but some dogs do have problems. Worm your puppy once he is settled into your home using a good product, recommended by your vet. Follow the manufacturers' instructions on dosage, which is usually on a weight basis. Thereafter, worm your GSD at six monthly intervals. If you have any worries or any queries, ring the breeder. If you have bought from conscientious breeders they will be pleased to hear from you, and they should be only too willing to help you in any way they can, with advice based on their experience.

Chapter Three

FEEDING

PRINCIPLES

Feeding is vital, not only to the health and well being of your Shepherd, but it is going to have an influence upon the dog's physical appearance. Although construction is largely predetermined by the genetic make-up of the dog, it is influenced, to some degree, by the way that dog has been fed and reared. In an extreme case, inadequate feeding could lead to rickets which would affect leg length and construction to such a degree that the dog might bear little resemblance to its genetic potential.

Feeding begins before the dog is even conceived, since conception will be influenced by the nutritional status of the bitch at the time of mating. Animals on a rising plane of nutrition are more likely to become pregnant than those on a falling plane, or in poor general condition. During pregnancy, good nutrition is essential for the healthy development of the foetuses, and after birth, nutrition will influence the growth and health of the puppies. Care with feeding is essential until the dog is adult. Once adult, a dog may be fed less expensive foods on a maintenance basis, but this will depend upon the activities involved; an active stud dog, or a working animal will require more than a maintenance diet.

FEEDS AVAILABLE

These days, there are three basic ways of feeding dogs. One is the traditional way of raw or cooked meat (often tripe) plus biscuit meal. The second way is to use canned food, with or without biscuit meal, depending upon the nature of the canned feed. The third way is to feed what is termed a 'complete diet', which usually means a dry food, though it can sometimes be fed in a moistened state.You will find advocates of each of the three methods, just as you will find owners/breeders who are violently opposed to a particular diet. You will even find advocates of vegetarian diets. On this last point, I would simply say that the dog is a type of carnivore which has developed into being an omnivore, and can therefore cope with a variety of diets. However, to feed a dog a vegetarian diet is quite complex, if that dog is to receive an adequate balance of nutrients, especially amino acids. I think that most dogs fed vegetarian diets are so-fed because their owners are vegetarians, rather than for any more logical reason. The morality of this is questionable.

TRADITIONAL: Tripe and biscuit meal is a diet usually based upon the stomachs of ruminants along with a carbohydrate, based largely upon cereal. Such a diet may lack certain ingredients, unless carefully controlled.

CANNED FEEDS: These can be the complete kind, or, more frequently, are meat-based moist diets, to which biscuit meal must be added. As with tripe, canned feeds have a high moisture content, which must be borne in mind when assessing such things as protein level.

DRY FEEDS: These are of more recent origin, going back over the past twenty-five years or so. They come in various qualities, catering for particular needs such as puppies, adult maintenance, lactating bitches, working dogs and veterans. These are the diets I personally, prefer to use. It is important to ensure that you are buying proprietary brands from a reputable manufacturer. There are many brands available which have been formulated following considerable nutritional research. Equally, there are products that are both cheap and nasty, and should be avoided.

WATER

Water is essential to life. You can last longer without food, than without water. Meat is made up of some seventy-five per cent water, and though you may not think of your dog as meat, that is largely what its body is composed of. Water is an essential component of muscle, and it is needed for the excretory system. The kidneys are involved in this, and they require liquid intake to function effectively.

If a dog loses too much water from its tissues (about ten per cent), it could well die. In hot conditions, a dog will drink more than usual, as a means of trying to reduce body temperature. Similarly, appetite is affected by water, since the utilisation of food does require the use of large amounts of water. Some diets, such as canned food, are basically high in moisture content, and will, therefore, lead to less water intake. But dry foods do require water to be fed. A hyperactive dog will probably have a high water requirement.

Some breeders in Britain seem to restrict water to their GSDs; and this is something which I consider to be bordering on the cruel, and certainly unwise. The theory seems to be that many GSDs have a habit of upsetting water buckets. I think this is only likely when they are not given water on a constant basis. In any event, it should not be beyond the wit of man to solve such a simple problem, without restricting water access. A dog should have access to fresh water at all times, and failure to provide this has no justification, other than selfish convenience of the owner.

A case might be made for restricting water to a puppy during the night while house training, but if that is your policy, the last meal of the night should be light, and you should ensure your puppy is allowed to relieve itself last thing before you go to bed. Certain feedstuffs will increase the need to drink (e.g. salty feeds), and if a dog has kidney disease or diabetes, it may drink to excess. However, such diseases need diagnosis and treatment, and the provision of water at all times is the safe way to operate. Excessive drinking, if it does occur, will not really harm a dog since the excess simply passes through the system.

DRY FEEDS

The advantages of dry feeds are that they do not require refrigeration, and they are balanced diets (if from a reputable company), and therefore you do not need to add anything to them. They are easy to use either dry or moistened, according to manufacturer's instructions. Usually such diets are sold in varying amounts from

An active GSD requires a well-balanced diet in order to maintain condition.

A GSD thrives on regular exercise, mental stimulation and good food. When you have found a diet that suits your dog, do not keep changing it.

The amount you feed a puppy should be adjusted in order to acheive the required growth rate.

small bags to 20kg (44lb) paper sacks. It is better to buy unopened sacks rather than to buy in small quantities. Not only is it cheaper to buy in bulk, but when buying a small quantity from a store, it may be measured out from a bag that has been open some time and may not be fresh. Stored badly or for too long, dry foods can become mouldy and should then be discarded. Never feed mouldy feed to your dogs, you could kill them. We store our dry food in plastic dustbins with screw-on lids, making sure that we empty a bin before adding another sack, thus avoiding old (and potentially spoiled) material at the bottom.

CANNED FOODS
These are easy to store (in a dry room) and to feed, but it is important to look at quality since some are quite poor (little better than offal), while others are highly digestible.

In Britain, the price of canned food is often related to palatability/digestibility, with more palatable diets being more costly. However, it is important to realise that many of the brands on sale, and seemingly in competition with each other, are produced by the same manufacturer, so that competition is more imagined than real.

Canned foods are not something we would feed as a routine, but we do keep them in store, as they can be very useful for dogs which are unwell or which seem to have lost their appetite. Remember that canned foods have high moisture content, and on a dry matter weight basis, canned food is possibly more costly than dry complete food.

TRADITIONAL
Unprocessed tripe is not a high-quality meat, but it is cheap. Dogs tend to like it, and it usually firms up stools. It is much cheaper than dry or canned food, but it requires to be stored frozen, which is an added expense. You need to ensure you have a steady supply, providing it ready-minced and bagged in lb or kg units, otherwise there is much work involved. Tripe is not something I would feed as a rearing diet, but I would use it as a taster, or as part of a maintenance diet for adult dogs. Some breeders are staunch advocates of tripe and biscuit meal diets, but such diets do need to be balanced with minerals and vitamins, and therein lies the difficulty. If you start adding calcium and vitamins, you can do it wrong and cause more harm than good. When feeding tripe, I prefer to feed it minced, not big chunks of tripe, which a dog could choke on. Note that unprocessed tripe is not readily available everywhere and the dog feeder should be sure of ample supplies before using this diet. Other meats can vary according to location and country. Like tripe, they need to be fresh and to be stored frozen. Failure to freeze fresh meat quickly can lead to it being contaminated by flies and other insects, especially in hot weather. Similarly, when defreezing for use, such meats must be thoroughly defrozen and used quickly. They should not be fed in a semi-frozen state.

DIETS TO FOLLOW
There are so many ways of feeding dogs, all with their own merits. However, in order to avoid giving innumerable menus, I will detail the diets used in our kennels. These have been used with both GSDs and the larger, heavier-boned, Bernese Mountain Dogs. All have been successful diets and should be followed as stated.

What you should not do is to change diets as often as changing your shirt. Some single dog owners treat their dogs much as fellow humans. Because humans do not eat the same food each day, they believe that dogs require the same constant change in their diets. Nothing could be further from the truth. The dog needs the flora of its gut to be fairly static, and constant diet changes can alter this equilibrium. Keep to a proven diet that seems to suit your dog. Do not chop and change.

PUPPY FEEDING: THE FIRST THREE WEEKS

At one time, puppies were fed milk replacers, and though these are still available, they are not used as frequently as was once the case. We avoid them as unnecessary. For the first ten to fourteen days puppies are blind and deaf, and they are interested mainly in sleeping and suckling. It is important that puppies gain weight, especially in the first forty-eight hours. There is evidence that puppies gaining weight, or not losing more than ten per cent of body weight in the first forty-eight hours, tend to survive. In contrast, puppies losing in excess of ten per cent of body weight have a high chance of dying.

Breeders should identify each pup by colour, using markers around the leg, or by different 'washable' paints, and every puppy should be weighed daily over the first few days of life to monitor weight changes. Remember that the rear teats tend to be the better ones for milk production, so try to share them around and do not let the stronger puppies monopolise them, as they will tend to do. Move puppies around to try to get uniformity of growth.

Supplementary food can be introduced from around the twelve to fourteen day period. We would use a complete puppy diet, which is mashed and offered in small quantities in a moistened state. A 'taster' such as a canned feed may be used with the dry feed, then gradually eliminated. Puppies eat from a large shallow bowl and soon adjust to this system, especially when the eyes open. When offering food, make sure the bitch is not around, but let her in later to clean up. The food is offered once or twice a day up to twenty-one days of age, thereafter increasing until the litter is getting feed offered four times a day, and staying at that level. Quantities are altered as the dogs grow, depending upon litter size and dam's milk supply.

FROM FOUR WEEKS

By about four weeks of age the dam is often getting irritated by the pups as they can do damage with their teeth and claws. Clip claws regularly to reduce the risks from this quarter. From this time on, the pups are primarily on to the complete diet, though they get some suckling of their mother's milk, and the only other addition would be water. The separation from their dam at eight weeks is not as traumatic with dogs as it might be thought, and most pups will continue to gain weight without any setback.

By eight weeks of age, a GSD puppy should be weighing some 6-9kg (13-20lb), depending upon sex and bloodlines. In general, bitches will grow at a slightly lower level than males, and the differences between males and females will increase with time. You should feed such amounts as are giving the weight gain that you require. Food should be made available for a limited period, and then removed. Fresh food should be offered at each meal. As the pups approach eight weeks, the diet can be fed dry rather than moistened, and then left to allow free access. In that event, check that you have not got a glutton who is getting too fat and if so, restrict its access.

ABOVE: The GSD should be kept fit and well-muscled, and should never be overweight. This is Ch. Rosehurst Chris.

LEFT: The nursing bitch needs large quantities of top-quality food.

In old age, a GSD will slow down, and will, therefore, need less food.

POST WEANING FEEDING

At eight weeks, the pup will travel to its new home. Having left its littermates, travelled in a car, and found new surroundings and people, the puppy will probably be a bit upset and may initially not want to eat. Offer your pup same diet as it was getting at the breeders, and do not introduce any changes. Dogs may not eat for the odd day, but no dog will starve itself for too long, so do not be in a hurry to change to some other feeding regime. You, not the dog, should dictate diet.

Your puppy should be on four meals a day (or free access), using such quantities as maintain growth, without increasing bulk beyond the limited puppy fat seen in dogs of this age. By six months of age your dog should be reduced gradually to two meals per day. If you are feeding dry feeds, then this should never be reduced below two meals per day. Ideally, these should be fed in the morning an hour or so after exercise, and in the early evening, again one or two hours after exercise – never before exercise. With dry feeds, digestion is better with two meals a day and bloat risks are reduced. If you feed tripe and biscuit meal, feed them separately as they digest better that way. From about nine to twelve months of age, you can start to change from a complete puppy diet to the next product, and I would suggest a complete adult diet, designed for the average working dog. Dogs should be fed these diets at the rate of about 60-90gm per 4.5kg of body weight. This is about 2-3oz per 10lb of weight. This is, of course, a daily amount so is fed in two halves.

I dislike having to weigh out food daily, nor is it necessary. If you know what the amount looks like when placed in a bowl, then it is easy enough to stick to that amount. However, your dog is growing in stature until some nine months of age, and gaining weight for even longer. The dog should be fed to maintain a steady growth, avoiding fattening, a bloated belly, and barrel ribbing.

ADULT FEEDING

We feed at about 8 am and between 4 and 5 pm, but this is not a rigid timetable. If dogs are fed strictly by the clock, they will learn to expect feeding and may start barking as time approaches. So not being strict on time can be helpful on that count. A dog in healthy condition and weighing about 36kg should, if active and being fed on a complete adult diet, be eating from 450 to about 680gm. per day or from 225 to 340gm. per meal. This is from about 10 to 15oz. per meal in imperial measures. However, individual dogs vary in their metabolic rates. A dog who burns up calories quickly will stay lean on the top level, while another may be putting on weight. You must, therefore, adjust diets up or down to maintain the right weight you require, or you must increase or decrease exercise. The levels given at the top end of this scale are probably excessive for many dogs, so you will doubtless be feeding less. Feeding is not just done by the book, but on what your eye tells you about condition and weight.

If you use another product, then feed according to the manufacturers suggestions initially, and alter these to suit your own dog. Feeding dogs is a practical exercise; it cannot be done from rigid diets, but rather by sensibly adapting levels to suit each dog. We have nine adult dogs and they all eat the same diet, but they have differing quantities according to weight, sex, status and exercise.

PREGNANT AND LACTATING BITCHES

A pregnant bitch does not need dietary increases until she is about six weeks through pregnancy, and then only gradual increases according to her appetite. You do not want huge puppies, with possible difficulties at birth, you want well-grown pups of about 680gm (1 1/2lb) at birth. At six weeks in whelp, the bitch's two meals a day can be increased to three, if she wishes it and eats up.

Some manufacturers produce a specific diet for pregnant and lactating bitches. However, we feed the normal adult diet or upgrade to the complete diet designed for dogs with a heavy working schedule, and give fairly liberal quantities. Once she has whelped, she should be fed as often as she requires and as much as she likes, so free access is best with plenty of water available.

As the pups start to eat solid food, the bitch may start reducing her intake. By six to seven weeks she will be largely weaned off the pups, and will probably be back to her normal adult diet. Many breeders believe in feeding calcium to their lactating bitches. On the correct diets this is not necessary at all, and may be dangerous.

OLD DOGS

As a dog ages, it will slow down in its metabolism and exercise less, and thus need to eat less. Some manufacturers produce a special diet for veteran dogs. However, this aging process varies from dog to dog; it is not a fixed thing happening at a fixed age. If your dog does show signs of age, then as exercise reduces, feeding should also reduce, since being old does not necessitate being fat.

Some pensioners do have clinical signs of disease, such as kidney or heart problems. These dogs need veterinary help and may require veterinary control of diet. Some manufacturers produce diets for the dog suffering from particular problems. These are available through veterinarians and some pet shops. Such products are valuable for the dog but you must be sure that your dog requires them, and is not fed them as though it were routine nutrition for all aged dogs.

Chapter Four

BASIC TRAINING

INTRODUCTION

If you have a dog, then there is a need to train that dog. If you have a bright, intelligent and large breed, such as the GSD, then the need to train it becomes even more obvious. A trained dog is a joy, an untrained and unruly dog can be a serious liability and, at a time when there is increasing pressure being placed upon dog owners, unruly dogs are the last thing anyone wants. In a book of this size training cannot be dealt with in great detail, since it is a subject that would fill a book several times longer than this. There are training manuals available of varying qualities, and you would be wise to invest in one of the better ones, and/or visit a local training club for instruction. Most large cities will have such clubs, even if they are not necessarily restricted to Shepherds. Nowadays, puppy playgroups are becoming increasingly popular, and if well organised, they can be very useful – provided your pup has been fully vaccinated.

Here, the intention is to outline a few elementary aspects of training, dealing only with those features considered the basics of instruction. There are certain principles that can be laid down, and these are listed below, although I am sure skilled trainers could add to them.

A well-trained, obedient German Shepherd Dog is a joy to own.

It is vitally important that a GSD gets used to a range of different experiences from an early age, so that it will develop a calm and steady temperament.

BASIC PRINCIPLES
1. Be consistent in the commands used. If you use 'Down' to make the dog lie flat, then *always* say that. Do not alternate with 'Get Down', 'Lie Down', 'Flat', etc.
2. Use short commands that cannot be confused with others. However much you may talk to your dog at other times, when training be economical with words. Remember also that the tone is important and should reflect the instruction/praise being given. Talk to your dog in a conversational tone and never shout at him. Some tough dogs will rightly resent being bawled at!
3. Call your dog by a name and keep to it. Your GSD may have a registered name that is several syllables long, but it will probably be called by a short name of one or two syllables. Always use that name. If your bitch is called 'Annie' then *always* use that in training; not 'Ann', or 'Old Girl', or 'Lass', or the multiplicity of names that you will find a dog called by different members of the family.
4. Make training enjoyable. Do not overdo it to the extent that the dog is bored. Do not try to do too much too soon.
5. Do a little bit each day, however brief. A few minutes in the kitchen each day is enough for a young puppy.
6. Be liberal in praise, and never hit your dog with a lead or your hand. If a dog must be punished, get it by the ruff and shake it, much as its mother would have done in the nest. It will rarely be needed, but discipline is essential.
7. Remember that you *can* teach an old dog new tricks, but it is easier with an old dog who was taught other tricks in its youth.

BEHAVIOUR PERIODS
In training a dog, we are seeking to modify behaviour and it is, therefore, necessary to examine the behavioural periods of the dog. Research in the USA over a long period of time established that dogs have specific periods in early life during which learning is, or is not advanced.

NEONATAL
This lasts from birth to about fourteen days of age. During most or all of this time, the pup is blind and deaf. Its behaviour is largely confined to suckling its mother. During this period it is useful to handle each pup on a daily basis, but during these first two weeks the pup is relatively well insulated against psychological damage, and learns little.

TRANSITIONAL
This lasts from fourteen to twenty-one days approximately. During this week the pup is moving from neonatal life towards a more adult system. The eyes will open around day thirteen, and ears function soon afterwards. The pup can now see, hear and walk, instead of crawl. Teeth are erupting and semi-solid food can be taken. The pup is now conditionable in the sense that it can develop the capacity for learning.

SOCIALISATION
This period runs from three to twelve weeks of age. During this time the dog will develop attachments towards other dogs and humans, even if contact with humans is fairly limited to the immediate family of the breeder. During this period the pup is weaned from its mother, and in the period around seven to eight weeks it will

probably be sold to its new owner. In this period socialisation is crucial. Pups should never leave the nest (in the sense of being sold) prior to four weeks of age, and, ideally, not before seven to eight weeks, but they must be in their new home before twelve weeks of age, or be settled in the breeder's home if being retained. Failure to socialise a pup by twelve weeks of age can have a marked and adverse effect upon subsequent character development.

JUVENILE
This period runs from twelve weeks to sexual maturity, which may be as early as five months, but is usually closer to nine months. By now the puppy is in its new home, but in the early part of the period it is not fully vaccinated. The puppy, therefore, needs to socialised, but not exposed to the risks of contracting disease. Most experienced breeders compromise by taking a partially vaccinated dog out of the home environment to socialise it, while taking care to limit contact with strange dogs.

Dogs that are restricted to kennel life after twelve weeks will be severely handicapped, in many cases. Often the 'pick of litter', retained by the breeder, will develop less well in character than its siblings, who have lived in homes and in a family environment, while the pick of litter languishes in a kennel. It is thus of paramount importance that if a dog is kenneled, it is also given lots of human contact and affection.

At the same time, during this juvenile period, a dog must be exposed to all kinds of experience: other dogs, other animals, different humans, noise, traffic, car rides etc. Correct socialisation during this period will result in great benefits, in terms of the correct development of the dog's character. Some dogs are inherently weak in character because their pedigrees are full of nervous ancestors, and such dogs are unlikely to develop the correct temperament, in many instances, however well they may be socialised. There is ample evidence that character failings, especially fear, are highly inherited, but there is also evidence that inherently sound temperaments can be damaged by inadequate, or incorrect socialisation.

Dogs vary in their characters, and hence, in the way they adjust to the family. Some dogs are inherent pack leaders, and as they get older they will express this leadership in little clashes with authority – yours. By twenty-four months of age, such a dog may be difficult to control, unless you have taken it in hand earlier. Properly controlled, these pack leader dogs are possibly the best dogs to own, but they are not suitable for inexperienced first-time owners, or those owners who are not sufficiently masterful.

Most pet owners want what might be termed an 'easy going' dog, who will be sound in temperament, but not an innate leader. Few owners will want a cowardly dog, and to this end, never buy a puppy if it cowers in the nest, or if its mother is fearful. A fearful dog is unreliable, essentially untrustworthy with strangers, although it may be perfectly good in its home with the family.

HOUSE TRAINING
This is known as house breaking in the USA, and this training will start from the moment of getting your puppy home. With skill, it can be done inside seven days. Your puppy will want to relieve itself after feeding, on awakening, and during play.

Teaching your dog to come.

LEFT: Command your dog to "Stay."

BELOW: Leave your dog, stand and face, using the hand signal, and repeating the command, "Stay."

ABOVE: Give the command "Come", and give a tug of the lead.

LEFT: When your dog comes to you, give plenty of praise.

You must, therefore, be prepared to take the pup outside at such times, and you must *go out* with your puppy.

Do not simply push the puppy into the garden and leave it there, or it will regard this as punishment. Go with your pup, and encourage it. "Jack, Hurry" will do, and when he relieves himself, give him lots of praise. If you keep using the command: "Jack, Hurry!" then he will associate this with relieving himself, and as an adult will usually respond to such command.

Some breeders recommend laying down a newspaper, and putting the pup on it to relieve itself, using the command. Gradually, move the paper closer to the door as the puppy gets used to using it, and then take it outside until you eventually dispense with the newspaper. A clever pup will soon learn, and will go to the door when he wants to relieve itself. Make sure that you are there to let the puppy out, or you will undo the good work. Never chastise a pup when you find it has messed. A puppy will not associate the chastisement with the previously committed error, and things like rubbing its nose in the mess are simply useless. If you do catch your pup 'in the act', then say "No!", scoop the pup up, rush it outside, and start the "Jack, Hurry!" routine, complete with praise.

TRAINING: COME

Getting your dog to come to you on command is the most important command it has to learn. From the very start, you must begin to give your dog a name and use it. If, for example, you call your dog 'Jack', then regularly use that name and no other. He will soon learn it, and when he comes to you on hearing it, praise him or reward him, although I am not, personally, a fan of feed rewards. Your dog will soon respond, and once he knows his name you can start to recall him with a command such as: "Jack, Come!"

You must insist that he responds, and praise him when he does. If he will not come, then repeat the instruction and either sit down or move away from him, and in either case, he will be curious enough to follow or approach. Praise him. Never chase after him, or he will learn *that* as a game. If he will not learn to come, then repeat the exercise with a lead, and as you say "Jack, Come", give him a tug to bring him towards you.

Once your dog is out in a field, he still needs to be instructed. If you have difficulties then an extending lead might be used, and on the command "Jack, Come!" he can be gently reeled in. Always, if you command him to come, make sure that he does. Do not give up on him, and always praise him when he arrives.

SIT

This is one of the first, and easiest exercises.You can start soon after your puppy has come to live with you. In training dogs, the custom is to walk the dog on your left. With your puppy, stand it on your left, and simultaneously say "Sit!" and press down gently on the dog's rump. When the puppy sits, give plenty of praise, and keep the dog in the sit for a moment. If you do this regularly, the dog will soon learn the command and will sit, regardless of where he is to you.

You can do it with the dog on a lead, in which case as you say "Sit!", you pull up slightly with the lead. Many owners train the dog to sit before it is fed, and this is usually successful, but it gets the dog to believe in a reward (food) for sitting, when, in reality, it will need to do that without reward other than praise.

HEEL-WORK
You can start this at around four months of age. If you are going to walk your dog, it is better that it walks on your left, with its head just ahead of your knee. Start from the sit position, with the dog on a choke chain, then give the command "Jack, Heel!", and start to move, leading off with your left foot. Give a short jerk of the lead as you move, and the dog will go with you.

Actually, first time, the pup will probably go ahead of you, as far as the lead will allow. You should hold the lead in your right hand, and as the dog bounds forward, turn to your right and go back the way you were. Command the dog: "Jack, Heel!", and give him a tug to turn him around. Walk up and down for a short time, trying to keep your puppy alert and walking more or less to heel. Then command "Sit!", and stop the exercise.

If you repeat this on a daily basis, in time, the dog will catch on and learn to walk on your left. It is sound policy to make heel-work sessions fairly short, finish with the dog sitting, and then have a play after each session.

When you use a choke chain, make sure it is on correctly i.e. with the lead attached to the ring that goes over the back of the neck. When you tug, the choke will then operate, and when you relax, the choke will automatically release. If you use the choke chain upside down, it will not release.

DOWN
Start from the sit, with the dog on the lead on your left. Give the command "Down!", and as you do so push the dog's shoulders down and away, so that the dog is pressed down. Bend down with your dog, to maintain the 'Down' position, then release the dog, giving plenty of praise. Repeat this a few times, and the dog will quickly learn to drop on command.

STAY
This can be divided into two sections, the 'Sit/Stay' and the 'Down/Stay', depending upon whether you want the dog to stay seated or flat. The principle is the same, but it may be slightly easier to teach from the 'Down' position. Get your dog on your left, and command: "Sit!" or "Down!", and then hold your left palm in front of the dog's face, and command: "Stay!", then step forward to a few yards ahead of the dog. Repeat the command more than once. Turn and face the dog, still holding your palm as a deterrent, then return to the dog's right hand side and praise – still in the 'Sit' or 'Down' before allowing the dog to get up and move.

The first time will not be that easy. The likelihood is that the dog will follow you. In which case, put the dog straight back and repeat the exercise. Repeat daily, moving only a few yards away, until the dog seems to be staying as left. Then, and only then, go further away.

Once the dog will stay seated and/or down while you move well away, then try it out of sight. However, make sure you choose a location where you can move out of the dog's sight, but can keep the dog in your view. The 'Down/Sit Stay' when out of sight is something that will come later rather than sooner, but by then the dog should be reliable at the 'Stay.' At the finish of a 'Stay' release the dog with a "Good boy", or some such release command so that he knows the exercise is over.

The 'Sit', 'Down', 'Stay', 'Come' and Heel-work are the main exercises for basic Obedience. They should be tried in short bursts each day, making sure that your dog

To teach the 'Sit', stand your dog on your left, give the command "Sit", and press down gently on the dog's rump.

Correct: The choke chain must be worn so that the chain runs at the top of the ring, so it will release automatically.

Teaching the 'Down'

Start with your dog in the 'Sit', give the command "Down", and push the dog's shoulders down and away.

Bend down with your dog to maintain the 'Down' position.

Hold your dog in the 'Down' for a couple of seconds, then release the dog, giving plenty of praise.

is never bored with them. If such exercise sessions are associated with play, then the pup will enjoy them more than if they are dull and arduous. Other exercises will come, especially if you get into competitive Obedience, but a useful exercise to teach is retrieve.

RETRIEVE

The retrieve instinct in GSD pups is not highly inherited (about twenty per cent), but it can be encouraged. Most pups will chase after a thrown object, and long before you start retrieve exercises as such, you should be indulging in play which encourages retrieve. In the house or when out on a walk, encourage play by throwing articles the dog knows and will, therefore, chase and usually mouth or pick up. Encourage this, and encourage the dog when it does pick up an item to "Come", thus starting the retrieve philosophy. We try this with everything from car keys to blocks of wood, and most pups will retrieve in a fashion.

You can modify this by hiding articles, intially letting the dog see where you hid them, and as the dog becomes adept at finding them, hide them without his seeing. A command like "Jack, Seek!", or "Jack, Fetch!" will stimulate the dog, and most enjoy the play. I do not, however, advocate using balls such as tennis balls, since I have known dogs leap to catch a ball and choke to death as the ball lodged in the throat. Nor do I recommend sticks. A smooth block of wood, or a small light dumb-bell with slim ends, will be better.

This sort of play encourages the dog to use its nose and instils a retrieve instinct. When the time comes to try in earnest, first teach your dog to hold the retrieve object e.g. the dumb-bell by putting it in the dog's mouth, giving the command "Hold!". Make sure the dog continues to hold the object, but in such a way as not to hurt his mouth. Once your dog will hold the object, it is easy enough to get the dog to pick it up and carry it. From then on, the command "Jack, Fetch!" can be combined with "Hold!", and "Jack, Come!", and finally "Sit!'', so that the dog chases, picks up, brings back, and sits holding the object.

These few simple exercises are adequate for most dogs and owners. If you find you have a clever dog and that you have some talents as a trainer, then you can go further into competitive Obedience, or even better into Working Trials and such areas as Schutzhund.

Many GSD have good noses, and the hide-and-seek type of game can be extended to make a dog start the rudiments of tracking. Throughout, work must be made enjoyable with lots of praise and lots of play. You can use toys with a dog but be careful in your choice. If you allow your pup to have an old shoe, don't complain when the dog demolishes your brand new pair. Try to use objects meant for dogs, rather than those derived from old clothes, since this encourages a dog to play with new clothes.

Always encourage your dog to play and to retrieve. If you are sitting together in the house, get your dog to chase objects and pick them up – but never go on too long.

CRATES (FOLDING KENNELS)

Collapsible steel-mesh crates are available in varying sizes, and from a variety of manufacturers. They form a standard part of pet equipment in the US, and although the British have been slower to catch on – with some people regarding them as cruel – most breeders and trainers find them extremely useful. The size we recommend is one big enough to house an adult GSD – 114 x 69 x 76cm (49 x 27 x 30in).

From the start, accustom your dog to go into the crate and stay there, but do not use the crate as a punishment block, since it is not, and should not be used in this way. With puppies, we put them into a crate when they need a rest, and puppies need lots of rest. If you feed your pup in the crate, your puppy will get used to going in, and regard it as "his place". This should be respected.

Children and puppies get on well together, but children can play too long for most puppies. It is, therefore, invaluable to have a place where the puppy can go to rest undisturbed. Even if you are at home all day, you will have occasion to go out at times and the pup has to be left behind. Young pups can get into mischief, not only chewing at expensive furniture, but they can also chew through telephone wires etc. We had a pup who chewed through an electric cable to the refrigerator – and, fortunately, lived to tell the tale.

The advantage of using a crate is that you can go out, knowing that the pup is safe from mischief and from harm. We use crates in this way, and we sleep young pups in a crate at night. When they are grown up we find that our dogs will go into an open crate of their own volition, to find some peace and quiet. If they regarded a crate as a punishment, they would avoid it like the plague.

EXERCISE

Dogs vary in the degree of exercise they need or want. Young pups are best exercising in their run, or the house, or the garden at their own pace. The occasional controlled exercise on a lead is undertaken more to socialise, than as exercise *per se,* as are visits to the training club. By six months, controlled lead exercise can be undertaken, and this might amount to a couple of half-mile walks daily. As the dog matures, it will need and cope with more exercise. A show dog that is being exhibited, and hence needing to be in fit condition, might be having running exercise several nights a week, and a couple of miles at a time.

Over-exercise does more harm than good, and excessive exercise of puppies cannot help such aspects as hip dysplasia, even if it may not always harm hip status. You need to keep your dog in a fit state, so an adult male needs to weigh 36kg (79lb) or thereabouts. The dog should be weighed at intervals, or you should judge by appearance whether your GSD is in a fit state, and act accordingly.

If a dog is too fat, it needs more exercise or less food, or more probably, both. If a dog is too thin it needs more food, a worm check or less exercise, if that seems to be excessive. Stud dogs, working dogs, and show dogs getting lots of activity, need to be fed well and exercised accordingly. However, youngsters under twelve months need cautious exercise, and should not be run for miles and miles.

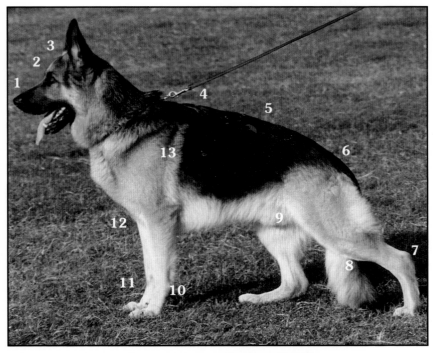

Anatomy of the GSD

1. MUZZLE
2. STOP
3. OCCIPUT
4. WITHERS
5. BACK
6. CROUP
7. HOCK JOINT

8. STIFLE
9. TUCK UP
10. PASTERN JOINT
11. FRONT PASTERN
12. FORE CHEST
13. SHOULDER

The German Shepherd pictured here is Ch. Shootersway Lido. The GSD is a dog slightly long in comparison to height, with a powerful, well-muscled body, giving an impression of strength, intelligence and suppleness.

Chapter Five

BREED TYPE

INTRODUCTION

All pure bred dog breeds have been selected over the years to represent a specific ideal. This ideal is epitomised in what is called the Breed Standard which is a description, in words, of what the breed is supposed to look like.

Breed Standards were usually drawn up by early enthusiasts of the breed, working as a group, and their descriptions have formed the basis of what the breed has been selected to resemble. Some Standards have been well written and intelligently drawn up, while others have been drawn up in a way that leaves many inaccuracies and deficiencies. The Standard of the GSD was first drawn up by the SV in 1899 under a group led by von Stephanitz. The original version has been revised many times (1901, 1909, 1930, 1961 and 1976), and each country has tended to use a version of the SV Standard translated into the appropriate language.

A grey sable, showing strong, masculine features.

A Standard is a kind of prototype of what the dog should look like, and it is up to breeders and judges to interpret that Standard. However, not everyone interprets words in the same way, and so differences of opinion can occur, leading to faulty judging and breeding. I will list each heading of the Standard in turn, and comment accordingly.

CHARACTERISTICS
The main characteristics of the GSD are steadiness of nerves, attentiveness, loyalty, calm self-assurance, alertness and tractability. These characteristics are necessary for a versatile working dog.

Good temperament is essential, and shy and vicious dogs should be severely penalised in the ring, and rejected from breeding programmes. Judges ignoring such features are doing the breed a disservice, and their competence is in question.

GENERAL APPEARANCE
The immediate impression of the GSD is of a dog slightly long in comparison to its height, with a powerful and well-muscled body. The relation between height and length is so interrelated as to enable a far-reaching and enduring gait. The coat should be weatherproof.

A true to type GSD gives an impression of innate strength, intelligence and suppleness, with the mental attributes to make him always ready for tireless action as a working dog. Overall, he should present an harmonious picture of innate nobility, alertness and self-confidence.

Without training, it is difficult to imagine most dogs fitting this picture, but the Standard emphasises that the ideal GSD is a calm dog of excellent, *trustworthy* character. It suggests a dog that is readily handled, but not one which is leaping over everyone and making friends with every stranger it meets. It also suggests a dog that is a 'defence' dog *not* an attack dog.

The proportions of length (front of the chest to the rear of the pelvis) to height (to the wither) are such that the dog is longer than it is tall. Ideally, the proportions ought to be 10 long to 9 high, although the British Standard does allow a range from 10.9 through to the longer 10.85. However, excessive body length is not desirable.

HEAD
The GSD is not a 'head' breed in the sense that excessive emphasis is often placed upon the head, almost as it if were the most important feature. Nevertheless, a correct head is of importance.

The GSD Standard simply calls for a head that fits the body. Thus, a very strong and large head would not be suitable in a small male, and a small head would be unacceptable in a big dog. Secondary sexual characteristics must be obvious, so that the sex of the animal is identifiable from the head.

The fact that the skull is defined as half the whole head-length suggests that long-muzzled animals are not desired. Similarly, 'lippiness' is not desired; tight-fitting 'clean' lips are needed, free from looseness.

The underjaw should be visible when the mouth is closed, and some evidence of a stop should exist, but it must not be excessive. Long heads are often linked to faulty bites and missing teeth.

EYES
The Standard is explicit in calling for a medium-sized and almond-shaped eye, so both a round eye or a large protruding one are undesirable. A dark rather than a light-coloured eye is preferable, but care must be taken to relate eye colour to coat colour. An eye that will look acceptable in a brown face might look lighter in a black face, and so colour should not be penalised to excess. In reality, eye colour is of aesthetic rather than biological importance. Claims that light eyes see better are without proof, and suggestions that light eyes are associated with greater intelligence are tenuous.

EARS
Ear-size is relative to head size, but they should be medium rather than large or small. Tipped ears as seen in Collies, and hanging (soft) ears are quite unacceptable as they destroy the whole appearance of the dog. In recent years, some dogs have ears which, while erect, are rather weak in muscle, and this is often obvious in movement. Although many judges like a dog to run with ears erect, it is not a requirement as long as the ears are firm, and can be erected as the dog requires. It is important to realise that all GSDs are born with hanging ears, and these erect during early puppyhood. Ear carriage can be erratic during the teething period when a puppy is getting its adult teeth.

MOUTH
The jaws must be strongly developed and the teeth should be healthy, strong and complete in number. There should be forty-two teeth, twenty on the upper jaw, and twenty-two in the lower jaw. The GSD has a scissor bite – i.e. the incisors in the lower jaw are set behind the incisors in the upper jaw, and thus meet in a scissor grip in which part of the surface of the upper teeth meet and engage part of the surface of the lower teeth.

Although the odd missing tooth would have minimal effect upon a pet dog, specialist judges tend to take a hard line on missing teeth, and dogs with missing teeth are penalised. In most Breed Surveys (especially in Britain) a missing tooth prevents a dog being given a Class 1 grading. As a result, unlike many other breeds, faulty dentition is relatively uncommon.

NECK
The neck is relatively long, but not excessively so, and it is carried forward rather than upwards. Long 'swan' necks are undesirable, and dogs should not move with the head held erect, because this will reduce their forward reach. Some dogs that have erect held heads have forward-placed shoulders, which is clearly faulty construction.

FOREQUARTERS
Shoulder blades should be long, set obliquely (45 degrees) and laid flat to the body. The ideal shoulder angulation between the shoulder blade (scapula) and upper arm (humerus) is said to be 90 degrees, but, in reality, a slightly larger angle might be more ideal. A very steep front assembly or a forward-placed scapula will restrict movement, but the most crucial feature is bone length.

As a trotting dog, the GSD needs a long scapula and a long humerus. A short

The GSD should present a picture of nobility, alertness, and self-confidence. This is Ch. Kurtridge Quando at Videx.

The skull is defined as half the whole head-length, so the muzzle should not be too long.

A dark eye is preferred, but eye colour must be related to coat colour.

upper arm will lead to the dog dropping on the forehand in motion, unless 'lifted up' by the handler pulling on the lead. A correctly placed shoulder should allow a plumbline dropped from mid-wither to lie just behind the back of the foreleg.

A well-developed chest should not be mistaken for a good front assembly; often, forward-placed shoulders are seen with well-developed forechests. Similarly, a steep, forward-placed front assembly may give the desired high wither, but this is not the correct way to achieve a high wither.

Legs should be straight, with the feet not turned out in an east-west pattern. The GSD should have an angled pastern – not a straight one as seen in most breeds. An excessive angle is a weakness. The GSD is not required to have a very deep chest, but it does need long forelegs. Short forelegs are not associated with good movement.

BODY

The length of the body should exceed the height at the wither; the correct proportions being as 10 to 9 or 8.5. Although 10.9 through to 10.85 is given as the proportion (length to height) range, the ideal should be as close to 10.9 as possible. In modern times, some dogs are too short in body and that is not desired.

The chest is only 45-48 per cent of the height and must not come below the elbow. Ribs should be oval, not barrelled, or flat, and should be long from front to back so that the loin is relatively short. A long loin is a sign of weakness in movement. Some tuck-up at the loin is needed, but not excessively so like a sight hound (e.g. Greyhound). The belly should be strong and firm, not flabby. This latter aspect requires the dog to be in fit condition, but some lines do produce 'flabby' bellies.

The back should be relatively short, with length coming from the front and rear assemblies as well as the middle-piece. Long backs are associated with weakness, and will dip in movement more often than not. However, an arch (roach) in the centre of the back is not wanted, nor should the croup start from the centre of the back. The croup is over the pelvis, and should be long and gently curved. Short, flat croups and excessively steep croups will detract from movement. Croups are best assessed when the dog is moving.

HINDQUARTERS

The dog should have a broad thigh, with good length of leg bones to the hock. Angulations at the rear should match those at the front if the dog is to have a balanced gait. Any imbalance between front and rear angulations will lead to crabbing (running at an angle, rather than straight) or to excessive pick-up of the forefeet or high backlift of the rear pastern.

FEET

Feet should be rounded, with well arched toes. Pads should be well-cushioned and durable, and nails should be short, strong and dark in colour. Most GSD are born without hind dewclaws, as this is a recessive trait and most GSD carry the gene in duplicate. If present, hind dewclaws must be removed, but front dewclaws are left alone. Feet are not always good in the breed, tending to be longish and hare-like, rather than round and compact. However, splayed feet are rare, although most dogs will splay their feet on soft ground.

GAIT/MOVEMENT

GSD movement, at its best, is a joy to behold. The flow of the legs, the firmness of the back, and the effortless way that a good-moving GSD trots, is a unique feature of the breed, which no other breed comes anywhere near.

Good movement is not, however, assessed in terms of speed but in terms of ground cover. The dog covering the most ground with the least effort is the most desirable in movement terms. In part, movement depends upon construction. Body length, back length, front assembly and rear assembly all have a part to play, and the co-ordinated gait will depend upon the matching of angulations.

However, movement is also a mental thing. Some GSD just love to gait while others, no less well constructed, are bored by the show ring and move without enthusiasm; yet, in the freedom of a field, this dog might move just as well as the outstanding show gaiter. Getting a dog enthusiastic about gaiting is thus important to its show career. Side gait should be far reaching with good hind thrust, the power coming up through the back towards the wither, which will lower only slightly as the head is thrust forward rather than upwards. The back will be firm with minimal up-and-down motion.

Dogs which paddle are usually not balanced in front/rear angulation, and the dog holds its front leg in the air that fraction longer to maintain the sequence of steps. From the front and rear, the dog will be sound.

Thus, the front feet will be moving in towards the centre, but with the leg straight relative to the foot. The faster the movement, the more the feet will be placed centrally. The rear pasterns will be straight, and more or less parallel, driving but not lifting too high when extended backwards. Rear pasterns should be relatively short, not long.

The GSD gait is epitomised by the two 'Es' of Endurance and Economy. A good GSD should move without effort and be capable of moving for a long time. To do this, it must be a physically fit dog, and thus, gaiting is not only about construction and mental willingness, but it also requires a dog that is trained, and in athletic, fit condition.

TAIL

The tail should be bushy-haired, and at rest, it should hang in a sabre-like curve. Short tails, not reaching to the hock joint, are rare, as most reach the mid-pastern. Slight sideways bends are tolerated, but tails which lift high in movement, or which curl, are to be severely penalised.

COAT

The GSD should have a double coat, consisting of a thick undercoat, and a hard, flat outer coat, which should be as dense as possible. Long-coats are popular among pet owners, but are biologically less acceptable because the coat is less weather resistant, and they are therefore unlikely to be successful in the show ring.

A popular belief exists that long-coated dogs are better charactered and easier trained. This is unlikely to be true, but, as pets, they may be better socialised than many show dogs, and thus develop better characters and are therefore easier to train. About ten per cent of GSDs are born with long coats, and about half the normal-coated GSD carry the long coat allele recessively. A long coat can only be identified at the six to eight week stage, i.e. about the time it is sold.

A GSD should look typically masculine (right), and typically feminine (left). This is not just a matter of size, it should be apparent from the construction of the head.

The GSD's mouth should meet in a regular scissor bite, with the incisors in the lower jaw set behind the incisors in the upper jaw, thus meeting in a scissor grip.

The long-coated GSD is popular with pet lovers, but frequently it lacks the correct undercoat, and so it faulted in the show ring.

COLOUR

The GSD is typically black or black saddle with tan or gold to light grey markings. Dogs that are all black, all grey with lighter or brown markings are known as sables. Wishy-washy colours are considered undesirable, blue and liver-coloured coats are serious faults. White dogs are disqualified from the show ring in the US, and would be severely penalised in the UK. This stems from the fact that white dogs are less acceptable as guards because they are visible; while as herders, a white dog is less useful. If you ever work a white sheepdog on snow covered hills you will see why.

Colours should be well defined and rich, with black unbroken and tan dark rather than pale. However, type is not affected by colour, and those judges who argue that a line-up of black-and-tans is marred by the insertion of a grey or black dog ought not to be judging. Colour is not type.

HEIGHT

The ideal height, according to the British Breed Standard (measured to the highest point of the wither) is 57.5cm (23in) for bitches and 62.5 cm (25in) for dogs, with 2.5cm (1in) either above or below the norm allowed. The American Standard stipulates 22-24in for females and 24-26in for males.

Increasingly, the breed has got somewhat larger so that a 25in male would look small in most show rings around the world. There is a need to reduce size, but it must not be done by putting inferior 25in dogs over superior 26in animals. Clearly very large heights (27in males and above) must be penalised, however good they may be in construction, but it must be done gradually, if correct type is to be preserved. Body weights will vary with stature. A male might range from 34 to 45kg (75-100lb), or even more depending on its height, but excessive weight will detract from the dog's endurance, and most GSD males would be in the 80lb range, give or take the odd pound. Females would be several pounds lighter.

TYPE

Before closing this chapter it is essential to mention 'type' which is a much used word in canine circles, frequently misused and more frequently misunderstood. Type is not about colour, nor is it about size. A 66cm (26in) dog and a 60cm (231/2in) dog could be of different colours, are clearly of different size, and yet could be identical in type.

Type is about proportions. The relationship of body length to height at wither, the length of muzzle relative to skull, chest depth to height, upper arm to scapula, and many other relationships and proportions are all features of type and must be understood.

The so-called British Alsatian of the 1980s and 1990s is of incorrect type because it has proportions which do not match up with those laid down in the Standard. It is, thus, of a different type to the international kind of GSD seen throughout Europe, South Africa, Australasia and Britain.

A judge may prefer a 62cm high male to a 66cm male, but if they are to be 10.9 then their body lengths must be 68.9 and 73.3cm respectively. Despite their size differences they are, in this aspect of proportion, of identical type. Whether they were overall of identical type would depend upon other proportions. Until you can understand proportions in the GSD, you cannot understand its type.

Chapter Five

SHOWING YOUR GSD

INTRODUCTION

Dog shows trace back to the mid l9th century, and they have grown from small mixed breed events held in tiny rooms to large events like Crufts Dog Show, which is held over a four day period and attracts thousands of pedigree dogs. Many people derive pleasure from exhibiting their dog, though more derive pleasure from winning, rather than just competing. Most breeders exhibit their stock as a means of showing others what they are breeding, while at the same time hoping that wins at important shows will enhance the reputation of their animals and their kennel. However, showing a dog is not an end in itself but a means to an end, namely the establishment of merit in breeding stock. If you are knowledgeable about the breed, and you are able to assess your dogs without prejudice, then you certainly do not need to exhibit to know their merit. However, to have the merit of your dogs established relative to the dogs of others, you do need to exhibit.

If you are a beginner, the best way to determine the merit of your dog is to exhibit it, though you must not necessarily accept the first opinion (good or bad), but look to a consensus view of several judges. If you find that you do not have a very good animal then continued exhibition is wasteful of time and money, and you are best withdrawing from the ring. If, on the other hand, you have a dog that can attain high placement or gradings, then continue, provided you enjoy doing it.

ORGANISATION OF SHOWS: BRITAIN

British shows are controlled by the English Kennel Club, and, basically, they are of two kinds. Shows can be either specialist shows, run by a GSD breed club exclusively for the breed, or they may be shows run by a canine society, and thus catering for all breeds or all breeds within the Working Group (in which the GSD is classified in Britain). The two levels are Open shows and Championship shows. At Open shows it is not the norm, among GSD exhibitors, to exhibit Champion animals, and the judges can be selected by the organising club without KC control. At Championship shows the judges must be approved by the KC, and there is an award called a Challenge Certificate (CC) available for the best animal in each sex. Any GSD which wins three CCs, under three different judges, becomes a Champion. Generally, there are over fifty Championship events annually for GSDs.

Classes start with minor puppy (6-9 months), Puppy (6-12 months,) and Junior (6-18 months), and then are a mixture of classes based upon the dog's previous wins. This culminates with Open class, into which Champions and most other CC winners are entered. You must enter your dog in the correct class, and in most GSD

Ch. Quaxie Vom Haus Gero, top German Shepherd in Britain in 1992. Do not get involved in competition unless you have a dog worthy of showing.

The GSD appears in a wide range of different colours and shades.

The white GSD is penalised in the show ring.

The black-coloured GSD is rare, but it is an acceptable colour according to the Breed Standard.

exhibitions dogs only enter one class at a show – though no limit exists on this.

At small shows most dogs are owner-handled, but at breed club events and Championship shows this is less true. Nowadays, most owners use professional handlers, which can cost varying sums per class, and usually additional sums if the dog wins a CC. There is nothing to prevent owner-handling, but most GSD judging involves much gaiting of the dog. Handlers need to be fit as well as skilful – not the ideal occupation for anyone overweight or past the first flush of youth.

NORTH AMERICA
THE USA and Canada have events controlled by the appropriate kennel club, and covering all-breed or specialist shows. Shows are given points, according to the number of dogs of the sex and breed present. Depending upon location and entry, the points range from 1 to 5, and shows giving 3, 4 or 5 points are termed 'majors'. All points count towards the title Champion. In the USA to become a Champion a dog must gain 15 points, with at least two majors under two different judges, and at least one point win under a third judge.

Classes are not dissimilar from those in Britain, but Champions enter a Champion class termed 'Specials'. After Open class (held before the Specials), all the unbeaten males compete for what is termed Winners Dog, and it is this animal who gains the points. The same applies to the bitches, and then Winners Dog and Winners Bitch compete with any champions present for Best of Breed. After Best of Breed is chosen, the Winners Dog and Winners Bitch compete for Best of Winners, and an award is made for Best of Opposite Sex. Thus, in North America, Champions do not hold back other dogs from winning titles, as they can in Britain/Europe. Moreover, in the USA it is BOB and Group, or Best in Show wins which attract attention. In Britain Group/BIS wins are not highly regarded by GSD exhibitors.

The GSD Club of America holds an annual show at which a Grand Victor/Victrix title is awarded to the top dog/bitch, and a small group of the top dogs are classified as Select, similar to the awards in Germany. This show has been going since 1918.

Many leading GSDs in the USA are handled professionally, but unlike Britain, this means the dog going on circuit with the handler for several months, during which time the dog lives with, and is cared for by the handler, who usually travels the country in a motor home and trailer. This can make dog showing, on a large scale, something of a rich man's pleasure.

AUSTRALIA
Australian shows are not dissimilar from British events in terms of organisation and classes, but a class exists for Baby Puppies (3-6 months). At a Championship event the best of each sex in breed can be awarded a CC. These are given points based on a basic 5 points, plus 1 point per dog entered, up to a maximum of 25 points total. Thus, a dog that is the only one present would gain a 6 point CC, while a dog winning against 25 or more would gain 25 points. A Championship title is awarded on winning 100 CC points. It is possible that a dog could win a Champion title, never having competed against another dog of the same breed, but this would be rare for a GSD.

GRADING AT SHOWS
In Europe and Australia grading is permitted, and usually required. This means that

in addition to being placed in order, dogs are also given a classification signifying overall merit. These, in descending merit order are usually: Excellent, Very Good, Good, Satisfactory, Poor, Ungraded. Normally an Excellent grade cannot be awarded to dogs under 24 months of age. Ungraded is usually reserved for dogs that are effectively disqualified as being highly nervous, or missing too many teeth, or with missing testicles etc. Grading means that the prize cards are less crucial than the grading. Although everyone likes to be first, it is more important with an adult to get a grading of Excellent. Thus, winning first with a grading of Very Good would be less prestigious than getting sixth place but with Excellent. Grading is not usually followed in America. In Britain the Kennel Club prohibits it, which is harmful to breed advancement, although it certainly requires a breed specialist to perform this skilled form of assessment. Most breed judges in Britain grade mentally even if they are not permitted to give out grading cards, and so exhibitors can be told the 'grading' that would have been given – if it had been possible to give one!

PREPARING FOR A SHOW
You cannot expect to just turn up at a show and exhibit your dog. In the first place, dogs have to be entered in advance, which means you have to write to the show secretary to obtain a schedule from the appropriate society, enter your dog, and pay the entry fee. This will have to be done about a month or six weeks prior to the show. For big events you will need to ask for a car park ticket, and will get this, plus an entry pass, to admit you to the show.

Your dog should be fully groomed before the event. This involves bathing your dog a couple of days beforehand, and combing and brushing to get the animal in good condition, as befits a beauty contest. You will need to go equipped with a bowl to hold water/food, as you are going to be away for most of the day, and many shows will involve round trips of several hundred miles. In Australia and the USA shows run by two different organisations may be held on successive days at the weekend, either in the same venue or close together. With long travelling distances, this allows exhibitors two shows (with different judges) for one lot of travelling.

You will need a show collar (non-choke), and a slim lead some 5-6ft long. If your dog is out of coat, it may not be worth going, depending upon the state of the dog, although some judges are more influenced by the construction of the dog than its coat status, which is, of necessity, transitory. At some shows dogs are benched, and you need a benching chain to fasten the dog on the bench. Most shows are unbenched, so you can have your dog with you all day. These are preferable to benched shows, which are a rather outmoded form, still preserved in Britain.

TRAINING YOUR GSD
Long before you go to a show, you will have had to train your dog. This means you have to get the dog accustomed to being handled by strangers, especially having its mouth opened to check teeth. The dog will also need training to stand in the show position, and to walk and trot around the ring. These days, GSDs are walked and trotted ahead of the handler, on the end of a long lead. Your dog will need to be fit, because gaiting may take a long time, and unruly dogs will get short shrift from most judges. Ideally, you need to join a local breed club and attend its weekly training sessions. There, your dog can become used to the show atmosphere, be handled by others, and be trained to gait and walk correctly.

A dog show is a beauty show, and you must ensure that your GSD is looking its best.

The GSD is a relatively low-maintenance dog, and a bath a few days before a show, followed by a thorough grooming, is usually all that the coat requires.

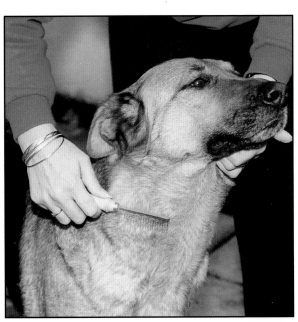

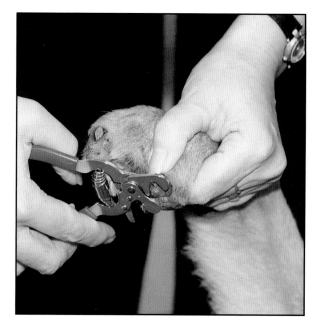

Do not forget to trim the nails so your dog's feet have a neat, rounded appearance.

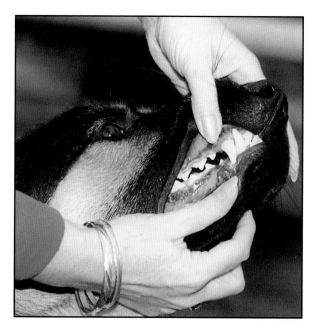

Your GSD must be trained for the show ring, and this includes getting the dog used to having its mouth examined.

COUNTING THE COST

Exhibiting GSDs is not cheap. Depending upon distance and counting entry fees, handler charges, fuel and incidentals, you could be looking at a considerable sum of money per show. If you win you get a rosette and/or a prize card, but there is rarely any monetary award. However, top wins like CCs and Champion titles do add to the value of your dog, and should increase the stud fee/puppy price of stock, as well as get your kennel name on the map.

If your dog is missing some teeth or is of dubious character, then there would be little point in exhibiting such an animal. Dogs that are the wrong colour (blue/liver/white), or those that are long-coated, or have only one, or neither testicle descended, are, in effect, disqualified everywhere. Technically, at least, in Britain you can exhibit dogs with such defects, but most reputable judges would discard your dog, so there is little to be gained by exhibiting such a seriously defective animal.

If you have a moderate dog, you will, perhaps, pick up the odd placements at small shows or under less qualified judges, and it is up to you if you persist. You can certainly win many prizes, but, really, only those at the highest level are meaningful. If you have a high-class animal, then you should be regularly in the first three or four places at most events, though occasionally you will run down the line for no apparent reason.

BREED SURVEYS

Breed surveys have been pioneered by the GSD world, first in Germany, then in other parts of Europe. In Australia and New Zealand they have been in existence since the late 1970s, and in Britain by the GSD Breed Council since 1991.

Surveys are not like judging, since dogs are not assessed against one another. Only adults (over 24 months) are surveyed, and surveyors are highly-qualified experts with considerable judging experience, usually appointed by the body running the survey, so not anyone can, or should survey.

Each dog is measured and each part of the anatomy assessed in a subjective manner, but based upon the Standard of the breed. Factors like hip dysplasia grades will be taken account of, as well as character and dentition. There will probably be a gun test (checking response to the firing of a starting pistol), and, in general, a comprehensive evaluation of the dog is made. At a survey dogs are classified as:

Class 1: Recommended for breeding.

Class 2: Suitable for breeding.

Not recommended.

Dogs in the first two classes can be bred from, but it is not recommended that the third category be used at all. Although Class 1 is higher than Class 2, sometimes a dog in Class 2 may be very outstanding but have a point too high on its hip score, or be a small amount over the maximum allowed height. The surveyor will make this clear in his report, and may give breeding recommendations.

Survey reports are published, with photographs, by the GSD Breed Council annually, and an annual survey book (Korbuch) is published by the SV; in Australasia the GSDCA and the GSD Council of New Zealand both publish survey books. These books are valuable sources of information for breeders, and essential buying. All would-be breeding stock should be surveyed, because it is largely through surveys, rather than shows, that we can make breeding progress.

Chapter Seven

BREEDING

SO YOU WANT TO BE A BREEDER?
Many people, having bought their GSD as a pet, are taken with the idea of breeding from the dog. The motives for doing so can vary from an understandable desire to have a son or daughter to carry on from their beloved animal, through to the highly dubious concept that a litter would pay for a new carpet, or the first instalment on a new car.

Anyone with a bitch can, if they find an agreeable owner of a male, produce a litter, but that is really being a reproducer of dogs rather than a genuine breeder. Dog breeding, and especially the breeding of large breeds such as the GSD, must be more than merely an exercise in biological reproduction.

Before anyone enters into the field of breeding they should realise that, for a beginner, breeding is not the 'lucrative hobby' they might imagine it to be. Producing a litter is easy enough, but rearing it correctly is another matter, and selling the puppies is often easier said than done. The 'lucrative hobby' looks less and less rewarding when you have a litter of puppies running on beyond eight weeks of age, with no apparent market for them. It is even less lucrative when you produce a genetic defect and find yourself in court as a defendant, being sued by the puppy buyer – and we live in increasingly litigious times.

ASSESSING YOUR GSD
Before anyone contemplates breeding, they should be able to answer a few questions positively about their animal:

1. Is my bitch (dog) suitable to breed from in physical terms?
2. Is my bitch (dog) of such good character as to warrant breeding?
3. Has my bitch (dog) been checked as having a satisfactory hip status?
4. Has my dog been tested for haemophilia A, and passed clear?
5. Is my bitch (dog) free from any obvious inherited anomalies? (see Chapter 9).

If you cannot honestly answer 'yes' to all five questions, then, most probably, your animal should not to be bred from. It may be that you are insufficiently skilled to answer questions one and two, which may well be the case if you are a novice. In that event, you should seek the opinion of someone who is experienced in the breed; such a person can be located at a local GSD club, or if you visit a few shows.

Be careful about the expert who is more self-imagined than real. In the main GSD breeders are a fairly knowledgeable bunch, but there are some who are not.

Before you get involved with breeding a litter, you must make an objective assessment of your bitch.

BELOW: Temperament is the first essential in breeding. These trainee police dogs respond to the command "Stay" – despite the temptation.

A GSD used for police work must be so reliable in temperament that it will remain under the control of its handler, even in the most stressful situations.

Be particularly careful of the advisor who suggests that you breed, provided you use his/her stud dog! It may be the best advice, but it may be biased and flawed.

If it so happens that you do have an animal of suitable merit in physical appearance, which has a good temperament, then you should ensure that hip status is checked through the appropriate national scheme. If it is a male, haemophilia A testing must be undertaken and the dog cleared. Even if your animal is good enough, you still need to brush up on your understanding of mating, whelping and rearing so that you can give any puppies the best possible start in life.

BREEDING CRITERIA

In some countries, certain breeding criteria are laid down by the ruling body (Kennel Club) or by the German Shepherd Dog Club. In several European countries dogs have to reach a certain status of hip before they can be bred from. If your dog does not reach this standard then you will be unable to register the pups, and, thus, their value will diminish almost to nil, hence there is no point producing them. In many English speaking countries, I think it is a matter of regret that no such rules apply, and you can register anything provided the parents are registered.

However, regardless of the rules that may or may not exist, a breeder should have certain ethical codes by which he/she will abide. No dog should be used for breeding if it is a coward or vicious. While it is not expected that a GSD will be everyone's friend, it is necessary for the dog to be of sound, stable character. The majority of pups, even from the top kennels, end up as pets, and as such they, like show and working dogs, must have sound, fearless characters.

Temperament is the first essential in breeding. If you do not have good temperament in your stock, then you do not have dogs worthy of calling German Shepherds, and certainly not worthy of breeding from. If you have got good character, then you must ensure that your dog is a good physical specimen, conforming to the Breed Standard. In most breeds we breed from about ten per cent of males and thirty per cent of females, so we need to be much more selective on males than females. Any puppies receive half their genes from each parent, and therefore both father and mother are equally important in litter terms. However, in breed terms, the males are more crucial because they produce more offspring and thus – used unwisely – can do more harm than any female.

In many European countries, Australia and New Zealand, and more recently, in Britain, GSD are breed surveyed as to breeding suitability. In some countries, the failure to breed survey invalidates the dog, but in others the survey system is voluntary. Regardless of the legislative status of the survey, it is highly desirable that all potential breeding adults should be surveyed.

On hip terms you should seek a maximum grade or level above which you ought not to breed.

SUITABLE HIP GRADES FOR BREEDING

Australia: GSDCA 'A' stamp (Normal, Near Normal, Acceptable, or Border Line). Use this last only sparingly.
Britain: Hip score maximum total of 30 (male), 35 (female) but preferably well below these upper limits. Breed average is around 18 and ideally you should select from animals below this level.
FCI countries: FCI grade A or B and only rarely C.

Germany: SV 'A' stamp (Normal, Fast Normal, Noch Zugelassen). Use the last category sparingly.
United States: OFA grade (Excellent or Good, and only rarely Fair).

CHOOSING A STUD DOG

If you own a male then, unless you use him on your own bitches you are dependent upon bitch owners coming to you. This is unlikely to happen unless your male is of sufficient quality to warrant his use. In this respect, the use of males is largely determined by the owners of bitches, and we can therefore concentrate on this aspect.

If you are thinking of breeding from your bitch and she meets the criteria outlined in the previous section, then how do you go about selecting the right dog? A breed survey should tell you where your bitch excels and fails, and if no survey system exists for you to use, then you will have to do it for yourself, or find a breed expert to help you. This is done by listing the virtues and failings of your bitch, doing this as fairly as possible – free from rose-coloured spectacles.

Those would-be breeders who can see no flaws in their own stock are destined to fail. No dog is without flaws, and one of the objectives of breeding is to improve on the failings of a dog, while retaining its virtues. This necessitates being able to recognise *and admit* to the failings. When you have drawn up a list of faults and virtues, highlight those of greatest importance, and equipped with this listing, go looking for a stud dog.

Ideally, you should go to shows/working trials as a means of looking for dogs of the kind you want. You should subscribe to the national GSD magazine of the country in which you live, and in such publications you will see stud dogs advertised. However, do not make your selection solely on the results of glossy advertising, and, equally, do not make it on the basis of pedigree. Many breeders pay considerable attention to pedigrees, extolling the virtues of particular bloodlines to such a degree that it is as if they were no longer paying attention to the dogs themselves. Remember always that a pedigree is never as important as the dog itself, and that you are not mating pieces of paper (pedigrees) but actual dogs.

Advertisments and shows should give you pointers towards the available dogs which might be suitable for your bitch. Your initial short-list of studs ought to be based upon the faults/virtues that these dogs have, relative to those of your bitch. Never compound a problem by mating dog and bitch with the same failing, but try to compensate. So, if your bitch fails in length of upper arm, make sure that her mate is correct in upper arm. If, in addition, he has a pedigree that includes dogs which excel in upper arm length, so much the better. What you must not do is use a stud who has an excellent pedigree for upper arm length, but whose own upper arm length is inadequate.

When you have a short-list of studs based on physical appearance, then look at the pedigrees and reject those who have pedigrees that are unsuitable to your bitch, or where there are possible problems that you do not want. Finally, go and see your studs and examine them. From time to time, I find breeders who have used a stud with a blatant failing (missing teeth, retained testicle etc.) and the bitch owner has been unaware because he or she has not checked the dog. If you are paying the stud fee, go over the dog and check him out first – but be prepared to have your bitch checked out by the stud owner.

A long-coated GSD is rarely mated to another, as the result would be all long-coated puppies, which do not conform to the Breed Standard.

Although long-coated GSDs are rarely shown, they are often in demand as companion dogs.

The success of the Guide Dogs for the Blind's breeding programme rests in their meticulous selection of brood bitches and stud dogs, and keeping detailed records of the resulting progeny.

Both male and female are equally important in terms of inherited features in a litter of puppies.

Make your plans long before the bitch comes into season. It is ridiculous to start planning matings when your bitch is still a puppy because her virtues/failings cannot be fully known. But equally, it is not sensible to start thinking about stud dogs the day your bitch comes into season.

You need time to plan matings, so do not skimp on the planning by leaving things to the last minute. Once you have found your stud dog and made the mating, it is up to you to care for the bitch and eventually whelp the pups (see Chapter 8), and by this time you have to hope that all your planning was correct, and that luck will be on your side.

MENDELIAN GENETICS

Gregor Mendel was a monk, working in the mid 19th century, who was a pioneer in genetic work. He dealt with simple traits which have been termed Mendelian traits, ever since his work was rediscovered about 1900.

CHROMOSOMES AND GENES

All dogs are made up of millions of cells, in each of which is a nucleus. In the nucleus, an electron microscope would reveal thread-like structures which are termed chromosomes. The dog has seventy-eight of these, or, more correctly, thirty-nine pairs. These pairs are called homologous chromosomes, and one member of each pair stems from each parent. This arises in the following way:

In the production of sperm (or ova), there is a reduction process whereby one member of each homologous chromosome pair is placed in each sperm or ovum. Thus, a sperm (or ovum) does not carry seventy-eight chromosomes but only thirty-nine, one from each pair. So when the thirty-nine of the sperm meet up with the thirty-nine of the ovum, we are back to thirty-nine pairs or seventy-eight chromosomes.

The decision which chromosomes goes to which sperm/ovum is purely a chance one. Moreover, the decision which sperm fertilises which ovum is also chance. With thirty-nine pairs of chromosomes, and with the possibility that a dog carries perhaps 100,000 genes, it must be obvious that a great deal of chance occurs in breeding. A breeder has no control over the laws of chance, but the skill of breeding lies in the accumulated understanding of the breed you are working with. You can never eliminate chance, but with greater understanding of the material you have, you can tilt the odds in your favour.

Genes are proteins, and a specific gene is always found on a specific chromosome at a specific location (called a locus). Because a dog has two versions of each chromosome (one derived from each parent), it can have two versions of any specific gene. It cannot, however, have three because there are only two chromosomes of any pair, and thus only two loci.

CONGENITAL AND INHERITED

Much confusion seems to exist about these terms. 'Inherited' refers to a trait which is controlled by genes, and, therefore, transmitted from one generation to the next. 'Congenital', on the other hand, means present at birth, and does not necessarily imply inherited. Some traits (e.g. hip dysplasia) are inherited, but are not seen until later in life. Other traits (e.g. some forms of cataract) are inherited and congenital (i.e. they are present from birth). However, some traits are present at birth (congenital), but represent manufacturing defects (i.e. something has gone wrong with the foetus during pregnancy) which are not inherited and will not, therefore, be transmitted to the next generation. Limb and heart defects in man associated with the drug thalidomide were congenital in that they were obvious at birth, but they were not inherited.

HERITABILITY

Geneticists use the term 'heritability' when referring to traits controlled by many genes. This measures the proportion of the variation seen that is inherited in a way that can be transmitted to the next generation. In another way, we can define heritability as being that proportion of the parental superiority (relative to breed average) which is transmitted to the offspring.

The following table hows some estimated heritabilities in GSDs which are based on published work, or estimated 'guesswork' from other species. These numbers are guides only, and should not be taken as being 'written in stone'.

Trait	Heritability
Back length	44
Body weight	40
Chest depth	54
Chest width	80
Fear	50
Hip dysplasia score (BVA/KC scheme)	40
Litter size	15
Muzzle length	53
OCD (Faulty conversion of cartilage to bone)	25
Panosteitis (Bone inflammation)	12
Rear pastern length	50
Thigh circumference	8
Wither height	65

HERITABILITIES OF GSD TRAITS (AS PER CENT)

These figures are estimates and would have errors of around 10 percentage points either side. Thus, length of back might range from 34 to 54 per cent in heritability, and litter size from a mere 5 to 25 per cent.

INFORMATION FROM RELATIVES

Breeders often place great emphasis upon pedigrees, but the value of a pedigree is limited in genetic terms. If a character is very highly inherited, then information on a dog's performance in that character is much more useful than the dog's pedigree. If the heritability is low, the pedigree and the animal's own performance are more closely related, but at low heritabilities neither is very valuable.

Stud dogs or brood bitches are best selected on their own performance for the trait being assessed, but if they have close ancestors that were also good, then so much the better. Similarly, if a dog has, for example, a good hip result then it is valuable to know his siblings' hip status. If siblings are also good, the odds on that dog doing well are enhanced, though they are never guaranteed.

MULTIPLE SELECTION

Breeders are rarely interested in just one thing. A GSD breeder wants a good

While a breeder may be looking for many attributes, temperament is the most critical factor of all. The ability to get along with children and other dogs is clearly important.

The GSD is required to undertake high-level security work in its role as a police dog, but equally important is the need to behave in a calm, sensible manner in all situations.

trainable character in his dogs, allied to good hips, excellent movement, correct wither height, and all the multiplicity of features involved in construction.

Achieving all these things is difficult, and the more things you want, the harder the task becomes. Some traits are genetically linked, such that selection for wither height would tend to increase body weight, and might decrease hind angulation. These relationships need to be understood, if progress in several features is sought simultaneously.

Breeders should always limit selection objectives to those of greatest importance, and set minimal limits below which they will not go. However, they should not discard an outstanding animal for a specific failing unless that failing is of paramount importance such as character/temperament.

When characteristics are positively related, improvement of one will improve the other. But when they are negatively related, improvement of one trait will cause the other to decline *unless* both are selected simultaneously.

PROGENY AND PERFORMANCE TESTING

When a dog is assessed on his own performance e.g. its wither height or hip score, then we are undertaking performance testing. The higher the heritability, the greater the reliability of a performance test as a guide to that dog's progeny. In essence, the performance test tells us what the dog *might* do, but not what he *will* do.

However, the measurement of progeny from a dog tells us what a sire *is doing* and, thus, is much more valuable than performance testing. The problem is that progeny testing takes time. If we assess a dog for hips, we can do so at twelve months of age (twenty-four months in the USA). If we then use him, we cannot assess his progeny until they are also twelve months of age (twenty-four months in the USA). By this time, the sire is at least twenty-six months of age (fifty months in the USA) after allowing two months for pregnancy of his bitches.

With progeny testing, we have to use a sire to find out if he was worth using, and if he is poor, we have progeny that we do not really want. To this end, selection on performance is essential, but a follow-up, using progeny, is desirable. A second stage of selection then occurs, with the poorer sires being culled from breeding in the light of progeny performance.

A progeny test is best done using as many progeny as possible from a large number of different bitches, and without biased selection of those progeny. If we use selected progeny, then we bias the results and may totally invalidate them. Always endeavour to see the progeny of your stock, both as puppies and as adults, and try to see as many as feasible – not just those winning in the ring. See them in different circumstances, and try to assess the faults and virtues which they possess, so that you can learn more about what your animals are producing.

INBREEDING

Most novice breeders are best mating their bitches to suitable dogs based on physical/mental attributes, with an avoidance of close breeding. In other words, type to type mating, with compensatory mating where one dog has a virtue, where the other is faulty. Mating close relatives is best avoided by such breeders. More experienced breeders might mate related animals (inbreed) if they have a full understanding of pedigrees, and if they are prepared to rigorously cull defective stock. Inbreeding, or the mating of relatives, should be done very cautiously. Such breeding will increase the risk of defects and anomalies, but only if such defects were inherent in the lines. However, inbreeding can also lead to problems of infertility, and lack of viability or resistance to environmental change. The novice breeder should seek to avoid close matings such as parent/offspring or brother/sister, and seek to have common ancestors only three or more generations back, if at all.

Chapter Eight

MATING AND WHELPING

INTRODUCTION
The dog is a fairly fertile species, and, under normal circumstances, about seventy-five per cent of matings should result in conception and a live born litter. Bitches which do not appear to conceive are not necessarily infertile since the failure may be the result of the owner chosing to mate his bitch at the wrong time. Then again, a bitch may conceive but 'lose' the litter at an early stage of pregnancy.

GSD bitches come into season about every 158 days, but there is considerable range (30-60 days) around that figure. Outside of these times, a bitch will not accept a mating, nor can she conceive. Male dogs, on the other hand, can mate all through the year. The period of gestation is around sixty-three days, but a bitch can bear a normal litter over a shorter or longer period to the extent ranging from fifty-six to seventy days, even though the majority will be close to sixty-three days.

SIZE OF LITTER
Litter size varies according to the breed, and in the GSD litter size can range from one to about seventeen pups, but the average size is around seven to eight puppies. A number of pups will be born dead or will die during the first hours. This will vary from bitch to bitch, but losses tend to increase from older bitches (fourth litter onwards). In breed terms, between eight per cent and twenty per cent of puppies born will not survive to eight weeks.

WHEN TO BREED?
A bitch may be capable of breeding from eight to nine months of age i.e. when she reaches puberty, but it is not normal to mate her at that time, although many breeders will 'try out' a young male when he is only around ten months of age.

Most breeders recommend having the first litter when a bitch is about twenty-four to twenty-seven months of age. This means mating her two months earlier to allow for gestation length, and it usually means her third season. However, it is important to realise that it is not *essential* that a bitch has a litter. Those who tell you that a litter is 'good for a bitch' forget that from many bitches, a litter would not be good for the breed.

OESTRUS CYCLE IN THE BITCH
The bitch starts the reproductive cycle with pro-oestrus, when you will observe a swelling of the vulva, and a bloodstained discharge. Hormonally, she has high levels of the hormone oestrogen, and low levels of progesterone. At this stage dogs will

Some breeders claim they can select potential show winners as soon as they are born, but realistically, you need to give the puppy a chance to develop, physically and mentally.

A German Shepherd generally makes a very good mother...

...but as the puppies get older she will want less and less to do with them.

show interest in the bitch, but she will not allow mating. Oestrus is the period of acceptance, and this will be about nine days after the first signs of blood discharge. At this stage, the discharge becomes clearer with less blood, and during this period the bitch will accept mating. At this point oestrogen levels are low; there is a sudden upsurge of luteinizing hormone, and progesterone levels start to rise. Ovulation usually occurs within the first few days of what might be termed 'standing oestrus'. It will last 48-72 hours, depending on the number of follicles that rupture. The luteinizing hormone peak is about forty-eight hours before ovulation starts.

WHEN TO MATE

Bitches need to be mated during or just before ovulation starts. Canine spermatozoa are quite long-lived, so a mating before ovulation might still result in pregnancy.

The first problem with mating bitches is actually observing when the bitch first comes into season. If you are late in seeing this, your bitch may have passed ovulation by the time you take her to a stud dog. If you own a stud dog then he may help you in identifying the bitches starting their cycle, but if he is not the mate of choice, you still need to take her to the stud at the correct time.

The second problem, is that bitches vary quite a lot in their cycle lengths. Some bitches are ready eight days after first starting pro-oestrus, while others may not be ready until day fifteen, or even longer.

Most breeders have to work on their own knowledge, plus any help they can glean from teaser or stud males. However, testing blood progesterone concentration does seem an excellent indicator of the best time for mating. To do this test you have to be in close contact with a veterinary surgeon, and it should be possible to take blood samples and have a reading the same day.

If the progesterone concentration of blood is over 12ng/ml, mating should take place within nine hours. This means that the test is quite effective, as has been shown by research undertaken in Holland.

In addition to taking your bitch to a stud at the right time, you must ensure that she is healthy. Venereal infections do occur, and many stud owners will insist that the bitch has been swabbed by a vet and declared healthy. In the USA stud owners usually require a certificate that the bitch is free of canine brucellosis. Without this, they will not allow mating.

THE MATING: PREPARING YOUR BITCH

Book your stud in advance of your bitch starting her season, and on the first day of season let the stud dog owner know. If the stud is in very great demand, as does happen with some GSDs, then the owners need to plan the dog's usage. It is essential that your bitch is wormed with a good product at the start of her season. She should be free of other parasites, since no stud owner wants his stud to catch fleas or lice from visiting bitches. She must also be up to date with booster vaccinations.

On the day of the mating, you will probably need to travel to the stud, since most matings take place at the stud's own home. The stud dog will be most at ease here, and, hopefully, a skilled stud owner will have a routine the dog understands and follows. If the journey is lengthy and your bitch is prone to travel sickness, do not feed beforehand. However if it is an afternoon mating, a light breakfast may be given .

SUPERVISING THE MATING

Stud dogs vary in the amount of foreplay they require, or indulge in, and the stud's owner should be able to predict the likely course of events. The bitch should be held by her owner at the head and shoulders to avoid struggles or snaps at the male, but a good stud will need no help.

If the stud dog owner does need to step in to assist, it is best if the bitch is facing to the left. The stud owner can then put a knee under the bitch to prop up the abdomen, and place the left hand underneath and between the bitch's hindlegs, to guide the vulva towards the right place. The right hand is used to take the tail out of the way, and then to guide the dog.

Once entry is made, the dog will start to thrust and the bitch must be held firmly at this point. The penis will swell and be held by the constricting muscles of the vagina. Ejaculation will take place; the dog will 'dance' on his hindlegs, and then he will seek to lift one one hindleg over the bitch, so that they are tail to tail and tied. Some dogs need help in getting turned.

Both should now be held still, ideally with the far side of the dogs against a wall; they must be prevented from pulling away or sitting down, as the dog could be seriously hurt. The tie can last from ten to twenty minutes, sometimes longer, depending upon the bitch.

A tie is not essential for a pregnancy, but most breeders feel happier if a tie is achieved. When the mating is over, wipe the bitch's vulva and put her back into the car. The stud fee is usually paid after the mating, *not* when pups are born. Tradition suggests that if the bitch has missed, a repeat mating is usually allowed at the next heat, if the stud dog is still with the same owner.

THE WHELPING: CARE BEFOREHAND

After mating, treat your bitch as normal for the first six weeks, giving her the normal feeding and exercise. Pregnancy is not an illness, and the fitter the bitch the more likely it is that the whelping will be easier and the litter healthier. From about six weeks, a third meal can be given at midday if the bitch wishes (see Chapter 3).

Long before the litter is due, get the bitch used to the whelping box and the area in which she will give birth. You probably need to start collecting newspapers for this event. On the day whelping starts, telephone your vet's surgery and tell them you have a bitch due, so that they are aware and potentially ready if things go wrong.

THE STAGES OF WHELPING

As whelping approaches, bitches respond in many different ways, but all show a drop in temperature from 101.5 degrees Fahrenheit (normal) to about 99 or 98 degrees Fahrenheit some twenty-four hours before the event. Taking temperatures is therefore useful.

The actual whelping starts with shivering and agitation, and often mucous comes from the vulva. The bitch may start 'bed-making' by ripping up paper as contractions increase, and she should not be discouraged from this activity. The cervix will dilate, and she may hunch and push against the box with constant turning to look at her rear end. Some bitches whelp standing, others lie down. Some whelp on the move, others in a stationary state. Some bitches are calm and composed, others are frenetic!

Long-coated puppies can be detected from six to eight weeks.

The aim is to produce a happy, healthy puppy, ready to go to its new home.

*An average
of ten per
cent of GSDs
are born
long-coated.*

Once straining starts, the first pup should arrive within ten minutes, but if two hours elapse with no result, then ring your vet for advice. The pup is born in a sac, which the bitch will rupture to extract the pup. If she does not do this, then you must step in and quickly clean the mouth and nose of the new whelp to allow breathing. If you let her chew the cord, make sure she does not damage the pup.

Alternatively, you can use cotton to tie off the cord, and then cut it some 5cm (2in) from the puppy's belly. If the pup is still and silent, pick it up in a towel and rub it to warm it. Still wrapped in the towel, swing the whelp slightly in an arc, holding the head and neck securely in a downwards position.

Once the pup is breathing, let the bitch be involved in licking, put the pup on a teat, and then wait for the next. In the interval between deliveries, change the dirty newspapers on which the whelping took place. It is a good policy to have a cardboard box containing a hot-water bottle wrapped in a towel or blanket. Make sure the bottle is warm, not red-hot. Then, as the next whelping starts, put all previous pups into the box to keep them out of harm's way, while still keeping them warm. When the next whelp is out, put all the pups back on the teats.

Between births, give the bitch an opportunity to drink, e.g milk with honey or glucose. If she wants to go out to relieve herself, take her out on a lead, and make sure you have a flashlight if it is night-time (it usually is), just in case she gives birth outside.

Whelpings can be like shelling peas, or they can take hours and hours, depending on the number born and the bitch's proclivity for speed. At some stage she may appear to stop and be finished. Sometimes this is a false dawn, and she may start up again after a lull. However, sooner or later it will be over. Clean up and put the pups back into a clean whelping box, using a suitable bedding material, such as the fleecy, washable type. Ideally, you should be close at hand for the first few days to ensure that pups are not laid on. My wife sleeps in a camp bed alongside litters for the first ten days!

SELECTING PUPS: POST-WHELPING
Once the whelping is over, have a look at the pups to sex them, and check that they are healthy and normal, and that all are suckling. If you have a defect like a cleft palate (rare in the breed) then it will have to be euthanised by the vet. If the litter is too large, then you may have to cull, or artificially feed the litter, or find a foster mother to help out. The next day take your bitch to the vet to check that all afterbirths have been expelled, as you want all such material out before the uterus closes.

ASSESSING THE PUPPIES
Some breeders claim that they can select the 'pick of litter' while the whelps are still wet, i.e on the first day. I regard such claims as improbable on a consistent basis. An experienced breeder should be able to select the best, but not that early, nor with one hundred per cent success every time.

From three weeks onwards, you will be sorting and evaluating, but puppies are constantly altering, and the best at three weeks might be less good at eight weeks. A beginner is going to need help at picking the best. Remember also that the 'pick of the litter' is just that; it does not mean that it will be an outstanding animal.

If you want to retain one puppy, only do so if you really feel it is worth retaining. It is easier to sell a pup at eight weeks than one at several months of age, which has turned out less good than was expected. Puppies have a certain value at eight weeks, but after that, value increases only for exceptional animals; for the others, value declines.

The intricacies involved in picking a pup would fill a book in itself, but, as a rule of thumb, do not retain pups that appear long in the loin or long in the back, as pups lengthen; they do not shorten. Look for balance in angulations front and rear, and if there is insufficient hind angulation at eight weeks, there may never be good angulation later. Look for soundness, character, and the way the pup strides and stands. Even at eight weeks, the sex ought to be apparent from the head structure, but features like croup and tail- set are largely guesswork at this age.

If you are going to buy an eight-week-old pup, ask to see the mother first. If she is a poor specimen, and especially if she has character problems, do not buy. If when you see a litter they huddle away in the corner, instead of rushing over to greet you, then turn around and go home. There is no future for nervous puppies in this, or any other breed.

Chapter Nine

GENETIC CONDITIONS

INTRODUCTION
In all breeds and all species, defects occur that are undesirable in that they are aesthetically unappealing, or they can or do lead to an impaired lifestyle on the part of the dog. In some cases these defects are acquired problems, caused by disease or injury, but in other cases the defect is inherited. No self-respecting breeder wants to encourage inherited defects though all breeders, however careful, will have their share of problems. This chapter does not seek to be comprehensive in respect of inherited defects seen in the breed, but it lists, in alphabetical order, some of the more common inherited defects known to exist.

BLUE COAT COLOUR: This is a simple recessive trait caused by the presence of the gene d in duplicate. Normal coloured dogs are DD, but some are Dd, and matings of two Dd (blue carriers) can result in GSD which are dd in genetic make-up. Such dd animals are born with a bluish sheen, making them look like sables which they are not. Most blues (dd) lose their blue sheen with time and end up black-and-tans or sables, as the case may be. They are not biologically disadvantaged, but are not normally exhibited.

CANCER: Numerous cancers occur in the dog, and it is believed that some of these may have a genetic basis and/or that some breeds are genetically predisposed towards them. The GSD, as a breed, is not particularly at greater risk of cancer than the average for all breeds. Thus, although dogs may die of lymphosarcoma (lymph cancer) or osteosarcoma (bone cancer), among others, the GSD is not at high risk for these cancers.

CATARACT: In the early 1980s juvenile cataract was seen in Britain involving a few dogs. The cataract was present in early puppyhood, and was certainly obvious by twelve months of age. The mode of inheritance was a simple autosomal recessive, but has a low incidence in the breed. Affected dogs should not be bred from. Cataracts in old dogs are part of the aging process, and acquired rather than inherited. The condition still occurs at rare intervals.

CHRONIC DEGENERATIVE RADICULOMYELOPATHY (CDRM): This disease is a relatively common disease in the GSD, where it is more frequent than in any other breed. It is seen from middle age (five years or so), but it can occur in younger animals. The condition develops over a period of months, usually beginning

Ch. Laios Van Nort: Top male German Shepherd in Britain in 1992.
It is vital to the future of the breed that only the best dogs are used for breeding.

with some hind limb lameness, but it is not to be confused with hip dysplasia since it is the spinal cord which is degenerating. The dog retains bladder control, but, increasingly, has difficulty with hind limbs becoming paraplegic. Most dogs are put to sleep as the disease progresses, but if left, there is further degeneration, loss of bladder control, and paralysis. The mode of inheritance, if any, is unknown.

CRYPTORCIDISM: Failure of the testicles to descend into the scrotum is termed cryptorchidism and can either be unilateral (one descended) or bilateral (none descended). Breeders often refer to unilateral cases as monorchids, but the true monorchid only possesses one testicle, whether descended or not. Such dogs are rare. About four per cent of GSD males will be cryptorchids, most of these unilateral. Bilateral cases are sterile, as the testicles cannot produce sperm in the body cavity. Unilateral cryptorchids have a reduced fertility.

DENTAL FAULTS: In modern times the GSD has tended to have good dentition, especially when compared with many other breeds. The most serious fault is an undershot jaw, which occurs when the lower incisors protrude in front of the upper.

This is exceedingly rare in the GSD (in forty years, I have only ever seen one case), as is wry (twisted) mouth. A more common failing is an overshot bite, when the upper incisors are ahead of, and not touching the lower.

EPILEPSY: Epilepsy simply means a fit, so that any dog which fits can be termed an epileptic. Essentially, the problem results from incorrect electrical stimuli in the brain. The cause of epilepsy can be varied; physical damage to the brain, cancer, certain kinds of poison, certain diseases, and even heavy parasitic loading, or teething, might give rise to fitting in some instances. All of these causes, and others, are acquired, and the dog should not fit again if these acquired features are corrected. However, there is a condition seen in the GSD (and other breeds) termed primary or idiopathic epilepsy. There is considerable evidence to suggest that this is an inherited condition, albeit complex in mode of inheritance.

HAEMOPHILIA A: Haemophilia A is a blood disease wherein the blood does not clot quickly enough. The condition is seen in man as well as many dog breeds. In the GSD it is of a moderate, as opposed to mild or severe nature. The clotting of blood is caused by several genetically controlled factors, and Haemophilia A is connected with Factor VIII. The condition is a sex-linked trait carried on the X chromosome, and there are five genetic kinds of GSD.

HERNIAS: A hernia is a protrusion of an organ from the abdominal cavity through an opening. Hernias can be inguinal (usually scrotal), perineal (anal), diaphragmatic (the diaphram), and umbilical (the umbilicus). Diaphragmatic hernias are almost always caused by injury, and inguinal hernias are so rare in the GSD as to be safely ignored. Although perineal hernias have been seen in the GSD, they are also rare.

Umbilical hernias, usually seen at or soon after birth, are known in the GSD, but at a low frequency of about eight cases per 1000 births. It is inherited in a threshold fashion and caused by several genes. Severe cases should be discarded from breeding, but minor cases might be used if the animal is of outstanding merit.

HIP DYSPLASIA (HD): The hip joint is a ball-and-socket joint, in which the femoral head (ball) should fit tightly into the socket (acetabulum). First reported in 1935, HD is found in many breeds and exists when the hip joint is badly constructed. Usually, the cause is a shallow acetabulum, but, at all events, dysplastic dogs can vary from minor flaws through to quite severely dislocated hip joints. In middle age, dyplastic dogs can become arthritic, which is a painful condition and a principal disadvantage of dysplasia. Although most research has been done with the GSD, the breed is by no means the worst affected. In Britain there are twenty breeds with worse average figures than the GSD.

The condition is inherited, with a heritability of forty per cent in the GSD. This means that forty per cent of any superiority (or inferiority) in the parents, in respect of hips, will be transmitted to the offspring.

Although excessive exercise in youth, along with excess body weight, might play a part, HD is mainly caused by genetics and can only really be corrected by breeding. Bitches tend to average slightly worse than do males, and during oestrus bitches can show looser hips. For this reason, bitches ought not to be X-rayed for HD during oestrus.

LIVER COAT COLOUR (BROWNS): Most GSD are genetically BB, and, thus, can produce black pigment even if they are white dogs. Dogs carrying the B genes will always have a black nose. Some dogs are Bb, and though they appear perfectly normal, two such Bb animals could give rise to a number of bb offspring. Such dogs cannot form black pigment and are liver-coloured, where they would otherwise have been black. This includes the nose leather. In addition, the bb combination causes lighter eye colour. Although biologically not disadvantaged, the bb dog is not normally exhibited. The bb combination does not affect non-black (e.g. tan) pigment.

LONG COATS: The correct GSD coat is relatively short, with an obvious undercoat. As such it is quite waterproof. Some dogs are born with long coats which usually, though not always, are devoid of undercoat. Such coats are less useful and more difficult to groom, but many pet owners seem to like the long-coated version. Thus there is not strong selection against it, though very few breeders would deliberately breed from long-coated stock. The normal coat is dominant to the long version, so we have three kinds of dog: normal, normal but carrying the long coat gene, and long. About ten per cent of pups are born long-coated.

OSTEOCHONDRITIS DISSECANS (OCD): This disease is one in which there is faulty conversion of cartilage to bone. The condition can occur in the shoulder, elbow, stifle, and hock, and treatment is less effective as you go down this list. The most badly affected breeds are Labradors, Rottweilers, and Bernese Mountain Dogs, but the GSD does have problems, usually in the shoulder or elbow. Ununited Anconeal Process (UAP) is a condition seen in the elbow, which is related to OCD.

Usually OCD is seen at around four months of age, with pups that are intermittently lame. There is evidence that it is an inherited trait, with about 25-35 per cent heritability. However, excessive use of calcium and rapid growth are contributory factors, with males, who are more rapid in growth, being more prone to problems than females.

PANCREATIC INSUFFICIENCY: The pancreatic gland is in the abdomen and secretes enzymes used in the digestion of food, particularly fat. The pancreas is also involved in insulin production. Exocrine pancreatic insufficiency is a condition in which pancreatic damage causes a deficiency of digestive enzymes. As a result, food is not properly digested. Affected dogs lose weight while eating large quantities of food. They produce voluminous, clay coloured, foul-smelling excreta, in which much indigested food is seen. With specific medication to aid digestion, such dogs can lead relatively normal lives, in many cases. Most dogs develop the problem before they are four years of age.

PANOSTEITIS: Excessive bone production on the long bones, often called bone inflammation. Seen between five to twelve months of age, it is an inherited trait of a polygenic nature, but with a low heritability (12 per cent). It is usually something which dogs grow out of in their teenage months, though it is a painful condition during puppyhood. It is more common in USA than elsewhere.

PATENT OR PERSISTENT DUCTUS ARTERIOSUS (PDA): This occurs when the ductus arteriosus, which is a foetal heart feature, does not close after birth. If it partially closes it is termed ductus diverticulum, and if it stays open it is called PDA. As a consequence of PDA, blood is not circulated in the normal way. The condition is controlled by many genes, and affected stock should not be bred from, even if they survive. The risks of PDA are not high in the breed, but are increased if dogs that are closely related to PDA cases are bred from.

PERSISTENT RIGHT AORTIC ARCH: The fourth right aortic arch is normally only seen in the foetus, but can persist after birth. This condition, though uncommon, is more likely to be seen in the GSD than any other breed. The problem results in constriction of the oesophagus, which results in vomiting, difficulty in swallowing, and often pneumonia. Unrelated conditions affecting the oesophagus (achalasia and megaoesophagus) also lead to vomiting in puppies, and it is important to seek veterinary advice to ensure which problem has to be treated. Again, affected dogs ought not to be bred from.

PERIPHERAL VESTIBULAR DISEASE: A congenital defect seen in the GSD, it is concerned with middle ear problems. Pups develop a head tilt and circle in an unbalanced way, holding their head back or to one side. Rarely do dogs totally recover. As adults, dogs afflicted with this condition will still show some degree of head tilt, in many instances. It is thought to be inherited, possibly as a simply autosomal recessive.

PITUITARY DWARFISM: Dwarf GSDs have been known for the best part of fifty years. At birth, they are similar in size to normal puppies, but by eight weeks of age they are very much smaller than normal siblings. They also have shorter muzzles, and are readily distinguished from under-sized, but non-dwarf siblings. Dwarf GSDs eventually reach a size akin to a terrier – 30cm (12in) – and then grow no taller. At about twelve months of age, the puppy coat is lost and no other grown, so that the dog is hairless apart from tufts around the ears and pasterns.

SOFT EARS: All GSD pups are born with hanging ears, which should start to erect in the second or third month of life. During teething, carriage is not ideal, but the majority of dogs develop the erect ear carriage, typical of the breed. Some have weak musculature, so that ears are not as firm as breeders might hope. However, some never get ear erection, and remain with hanging (soft) ears. This is another simple recessive trait, in which soft ears to soft ears would give 100 per cent soft ears. Most breeders reject soft-eared dogs from their breeding programme.

VON WILLEBRANDS DISEASE (VWD): This is a blood disease affecting Factor VIII, leading to symptoms which include mucosal bleeding. Inherited as a dominant condition from the gene VWD, with VWD/VWD being lethal, VWD/vwd being affected in varying degrees, and vwd/vwd being normal. Clinical severity declines with age. The disease requires blood testing by skilled laboratories to distinguish it from other defects.

Although it has, allegedly, been seen in Britain, it is believed to be quite common in the USA where a prevalence of twenty per cent has been suggested. In the USA schemes exist to test GSDs for this condition. Unlike Haemophilia A, which also affects Factor VIII, VWD is seen in both sexes, as it is autosomal and not sex-linked.

Whether you want a show dog or a companion, the German Shepherd should be sound in mind and body.

WHITE COAT COLOUR: White dogs have been frowned upon from the start of the breed. There are some logical reasons for this. As a herding breed, white is not an ideal colour since a white dog is not readily visible in snow covered terrain, and sheep respond better to coloured dogs. As a guard dog, a white animal is too visible at night to be desirable. On the other hand, white would be ideal for a guide dog, and for livestock protection work. However, the latter is not a trait seen in the GSD, while guide dog companies select on working ability not coat colour.

These reasons apart, there are no biological disadvantages concerning white coats in the GSD. However, because selection has been practiced against white for many decades, few of the top sires carry white factors. This means that breeders specialising in whites are disadvantaged by having a limited selection available. White dogs are, thus, likely to be inferior specimens.